CAPITALISM'S HOLOCAUST
OF ANIMALS

ALSO AVAILABLE FROM BLOOMSBURY

Posthuman Glossary, ed. Rosi Braidotti and Maria Hlavajova
The History of Animals: A Philosophy, Oxana Timofeeva
Philosophical Posthumanism, Francesca Ferrando
Principles of Non-Philosophy, François Laruelle
Philosophies of Difference: A Critical Introduction to Non-Philosophy,
François Laruelle

CAPITALISM'S HOLOCAUST OF ANIMALS

A Non-Marxist Critique of Capital, Philosophy and Patriarchy

KATERINA KOLOZOVA

BLOOMSBURY ACADEMIC
LONDON • NEW YORK • OXFORD • NEW DELHI • SYDNEY

BLOOMSBURY ACADEMIC
Bloomsbury Publishing Plc
50 Bedford Square, London, WC1B 3DP, UK
1385 Broadway, New York, NY 10018, USA
29 Earlsfort Terrace, Dublin 2, Ireland

BLOOMSBURY, BLOOMSBURY ACADEMIC and the Diana logo are
trademarks of Bloomsbury Publishing Plc

First published in Great Britain 2020
Paperback edition first published 2021

Copyright © Katerina Kolozova, 2020

Katerina Kolozova has asserted her right under the Copyright,
Designs and Patents Act, 1988, to be identified as Author of this work.

For legal purposes the Acknowledgements on p. x constitute
an extension of this copyright page.

Cover design by Maria Rajka
Cover image © Artisticco LLC / Alamy Stock Vector

All rights reserved. No part of this publication may be reproduced or
transmitted in any form or by any means, electronic or mechanical,
including photocopying, recording, or any information storage or retrieval
system, without prior permission in writing from the publishers.

Bloomsbury Publishing Plc does not have any control over, or responsibility for,
any third-party websites referred to or in this book. All internet addresses given
in this book were correct at the time of going to press. The author and publisher
regret any inconvenience caused if addresses have changed or sites have
ceased to exist, but can accept no responsibility for any such changes.

A catalogue record for this book is available from the British Library.

A catalog record for this book is available from the Library of Congress.

ISBN: HB: 978-1-3501-0968-1
PB: 978-1-3502-5357-5
ePDF: 978-1-3501-0967-4
eBook: 978-1-3501-0969-8

Typeset by Integra Software Services Pvt. Ltd.

To find out more about our authors and books visit
www.bloomsbury.com and sign up for our newsletters.

CONTENTS

Foreword by John Ó Maoilearca: "Holocaust Denial" vi
Acknowledgements x

Introduction 1

1 The physical and the automaton, introducing the radical dyad of the non-human 29

2 Formalism of materialist reason 55

3 Subjectivity as inherently philosophical entity and the third person's perspective 89

4 Homologies and asymmetries between the automata of capital and patriarchy 113

5 New political economy is possible only under the condition of abolishment of the metaphysics of animal-for-killing 135

List of References 152
Index 157

FOREWORD BY JOHN Ó MAOILEARCA: "HOLOCAUST DENIAL"

I can only repay the honor of writing these first words to Katerina Kolozova's astonishing book by citing its last words:

> Humanity is treated in its identity in the last instance as one among the many phenomena in the vast out-there without assigning it any special status. In doing so, we have to start by coming to terms with what we did to the animals in the constitutive act of philosophy.

She ends her work with an imperative for us to begin anew, with the demand that we "start by coming to terms." Yet it is this "coming to terms," as both acknowledgment of fact and acceptance of affect, that is the hardest thing for a so-called human to *begin*, no matter to complete. "Holocaust" can be an emotive word, after all. A classicist by training, Kolozova is concerned firstly with the original and etymological meaning of "holocaust" for the Ancient Greeks—as *Holocaustos*, the "burning of the dead animal" (which ensures the "immortal light of reason"). Yet contemporary connotations will always bring more recent history to mind. And this is when "Holocaust" becomes a divisive term in the comparison between human and non-human suffering. In *The Lives of Animals* (1999), J. M. Coetzee dramatises the divisions it creates through an encounter between an animal advocate who makes the parallel between atrocities committed by the National Socialist government of Germany in the 1940s, and an academic, the latter arguing that the advocate has made an immoral analogy:

You took over for your own purposes the familiar comparison between the murdered Jews of Europe and slaughtered cattle. The Jews died like cattle, therefore cattle die like Jews, you say. That is a trick with words which I will not accept. You misunderstand the nature of likenesses. (pp. 49–50)

Here is a perfect *differend*: for one, it is the analogy which is immoral; for the other, it is the disanalogy which is evil. That the first accuser is Jewish makes it all the more dramatic in Coetzee's book, though still inessential: it was Isaac Bashevis Singer who wrote that, with respect to animals, "all people are Nazis" and that "for animals it is an eternal Treblinka" (thus giving the title to Charles Patterson's book, *Eternal Treblinka*, in 2002). Nobody wants to be called a "Nazi" (even some Nazis no doubt). As the *reductio* of every heated argument, the term "Nazi" has become an emotive speech act, emptied of any historical significance in favor of its performative force—whoever declares it first is, at a minimum, not a Nazi. Not the perpetrator of a Holocaust. Though it may not make her a righteous soul either (as, say, some vegans are accused of), at least one is proven to be the least-worst: not-Nazi. Announcing and accepting the Animal Holocaust, however ("coming to terms"), thwarts any retreat to such a safe space.

Though Kolozova herself makes no direct analogy between the Jewish holocaust and the animal one, the original function of *Holocaustos*—the "burning of the dead animal"—as the "foundation of *logos* and law and order in the polis," has implications that are even more terrifying. In what Derrida called our "war on animals," we are all criminals, most often unconsciously—simply "following" the orders and laws of the polis.

So denial is normal, standard even. The word "denial" comes from *denyance*, meaning "unconscious suppression of painful or embarrassing feelings." Freudians say that we are "in denial"—a matter of affect more than conscious decision. This is not a question of denial of numbers: how many killed?—or of comparison: whose Holocaust was worst, or first, in some kind of bleeding or wound-measuring contest—"my wound is larger (deeper, more enduring, more irreparable, more essentially Modern ... etc.) than your wound." It is a matter of the bodily affect that comes with "*coming to terms.*" Memorial is not enough: one might well remember one Holocaust in order to deny (forget or not see) a hundred others. For François Laruelle's Non-Philosophical stance, the Victim is a central figure, but only as who or what is not recorded by the "World." Philosophy is the gesture of thought that decides who is a victim and who is not, within its World. Yet the victim of Philosophy is always "the repression of another victim, too obvious to not be forgotten or unnoticed." Non-Philosophy, the thought that Kolozova practices here with this book, is interested in those victims who reside within philosophy's structural blind spot, those unheard, unrecorded, unacknowledged: the unknown that cannot be categorised by Philosophy. This is why Kolozova's final words also refer to "what we did to the animals in the constitutive act of philosophy." This is not about economics, party politics, or even speciesism: it is the gesture in thought, called Philosophy, that enacts the possibility of hierarchy, of all inequality—who is counted and who is not, who is a (human) person, and who is not. Everything else, from cheap food policies on one side through to green politics on the other, are consequences of this. That is also why the *resistance* to the non-philosophical approach is so acute: its attempt to see all things equally, living and non-living, all species, all races, all genders, in a global (or rather unWorlding) gesture, runs wholly counter to the founding act of *any* philosophical thought, which is *to make unequal*. Philosophy is not *a* thought *about* inequality; *it is the generative act of inequality in thought, and therewith in the World (the Thought-World of Capitalism)*.

That is why so much of Kolozova's work here concerns Marx, Lacan, Haraway, and, of course, Laruelle: because any rival to Capitalism's regime of material exploitation begins with *the* philosophical thought—inequality. Not that Kolozova is then permanently set upon the moral high ground as a result of her book: philosophical inequality is not a personal decision but a constant threat within thinking, one that harasses all of us continually. She is no righteous soul. That is also why this book is not filled with examples, or images, of animal exploitation, as if any finite number of cases or pictures might make the denial of an Animal Holocaust impossible. Do we need more of them in order to believe, to accept? What *Capitalism's Holocaust of Animals* is tackling here is the mode of thinking that makes any such exploitation, the thought of inequality possible: "The complete holocaust of all animal life will insure the complete rule of pure reason." Kolozova's earlier book, *The Lived Revolution*, spoke of a solidarity with any "body in pain" shared by human and non-human animal alike. Her new book is a practice of such thoughtful solidarity, a thinking in terms of the Real that ties together even more closely the effects of Philosophy and Capitalism ("capitalism-as-philosophy") upon the suffering animal body (human and non-human). Though less severe, "denial" is also a form of pain: the revolutionary struggles against speciesism, sexism, and racism are not designed to create new types of personal (moral) superiority but to free all our thinking from viciousness. By "coming to terms with what *we* did," by accepting the Holocaust, Kolozova denies only the denial—and what she affirms is the equality of the living.

ACKNOWLEDGEMENTS

I would like to thank my friends and colleagues for inspiring me to address the main topics of this book as well as to experiment with particular methodological combinations. Rick Elmore has made it apparent to me that my previous book, *Toward Radical Metaphysics of Socialism* (2015), could lead only to something close to animal studies or a treatment of capitalism that inevitably tackles the problem of the animal at the center of the political-economic paradigm of our global era. He also pointed out to me how important it would be to do so by way of resorting to the method of non-philosophy. I thank John Ó Maoilearca for the establishment of the "animal line" inside the tradition (in making) of non-philosophy, or of the non-standard philosophy, and for the concept of the non-human that is the central explanatory instrument of this book. Many thanks to François Laruelle for the constant inspiration and support, but even more importantly, for his friendship. I am expressing my gratefulness and sense of deep friendship to Anne Françoise Schmid whose constant support as a friend and as a colleague has been relentless throughout the years. Special thanks go to Taylor Adkins for his keen and precise oversight of my language and the tidiness of my Anglophone non-philosophical expression. I owe thanks to the New Centre for Research and Practice (Grand Rapids/Seattle, MI) for providing me with a platform of advanced students with whom I have been able to exchange ideas and test the viability and communicability of my theses during the development and the completion of this manuscript. I would also like to thank Iris van Tuin and Rosi Braidotti for having included me in a number of projects whose ideas have sparked some of the questions I raise here and my responses are perhaps a continuation of the discussions we had in person preceding this manuscript. I believe I owe special thanks to Dominic

Fox whose polemical exchange with me in the online Philosophy Symposium curated by Rick Elmore has inspired the second chapter of this book. My other interlocutors in that symposium, Miglena Nikolchina and Anthony Paul Smith, have provided me with reasons and prescripts to foreground modes of not being dismissive of the concerns of those habitually protected in terms of identity politics while continuing to pursue a possibility of a feminist discourse beyond the epistemic presuppositions of post-structuralism. Many thanks to Etienne Brouzes for his visual representation of the double determination in the last instance.

I thank my family and friends for their support, but most of all my daughter Isidora Hennig. To her I am dedicating this book, with all my love. By extension, it is also dedicated to all the animals we—Isidora and I—have saved from pain or death and all the animals that still await our help, especially the mothers among them and their little ones. Finally, I thank my sister, Kristina, for her relentless and uncompromising commitment to building a more just world for the animals and women and children of this planet, and for serving as my constant activist inspiration.

Berlin, August 2018

Introduction

From the post-human to the non-human

For decades, the project of post-humanism has been dedicated to the transcendence of the human as metaphysical-ideological creation of the post-Enlightenment anthropocentrism. It seems to rely mainly on the post-structuralist methodological apparatus and, in that sense, it represents an attempt toward deployment of the full political and philosophical potential of Foucault's declaration "Man is dead." This exclamation is Foucault's invitation that we examine and admit the limits of the modern paradigm of anthropocentrism. It is neither a call toward its transcendence, toward moving to the next stage of development and arriving at a status of a superhuman, nor is it a nihilist realisation. It merely points to the historical limits of the paradigm, as well as to the fallacy of treating humanism as the self-evident post-metaphysical gravitational center of thought and political reality. Considering that, according to Foucault, there is no progressional continuity in the change of epistemic paradigms, one might ask if transcendence of metaphysics would have to be the necessary development of the process of abandonment of the humanist paradigm. What would be transcended is the illusory self-evidence of what being human means and its post-Enlightenment presumptions (Foucault, 1966: 346–360). Throughout his opus, and more specifically in his considerations of biopolitics or the control and exploitation of life and death, Foucault committed to a philosophical and political rehabilitation of the body. In Foucault, life and physicality have come to occupy the place previously held by the now evacuated specter of humanism. Foucault's project is post-humanist, not post-human. The human in its aspects of life and physicality, determined by the body, is to be salvaged and becomes the fundament of his or her "care of the self." The center of gravity has been pushed toward human animality.

Similarly, Donna Haraway has been insisting on a post-humanism with an animal face establishing a physical and transcendental continuum with technology. In her "Manifesto for Cyborgs: Science, Technology, and Socialist Feminism in the 1980's" (Haraway, 1985: 65–108), building on one of the fundamental tenets of the socialist utopia, Haraway urges the subjugated bodies and decentered selves of the post-humanist era to seize the means of production (not her words but my interpretation): admitting that the origin of contemporary technological development lies in capitalist militarism, she insists that the animal the human has always been becomes essentially and unavoidably hybridised with technology, that this dyad is the essence of the post-human she later renamed "the inhuman" (Haraway, 2015: 160). Post-humanism, as the result of its own "philosophical spontaneity" (Laruelle), attempts to reconcile the two of the radical dyad of technology and the animal by way of proposing some sort of a resolution of the opposition, a dialectical outcome—a unity of some sort. The (post)human is a "hybrid," a unified duality, in which the element of intellect holds a superior and exploitative position vis-à-vis its prelingual counterpart, the body. Therefore, the automated self is what the dyad amounts to in most of the post-humanist visions of society. Such seems to be Rosi Braidotti's and Katherine Hayles's (1999) vision of the future post-human self—in spite of the sensibility toward human animalism and the animals, "becoming posthuman" seems to be the next evolutionary but also revolutionary step.

> There is another fundamental problem with the residual humanism of the analytically posthuman attempts to moralize technology and sideline experiments with new forms of subjectivity, namely their over-confidence about the moral intentionality of the technology itself. More specifically, they neglect the current state of autonomy reached by the machines. The complexity of our smart technologies lies at the core of the post-anthropocentric turn. (Braidotti, 2013: 43)

This is an example of what pervades contemporary post-humanism, as demonstrated by Cary Wolfe in his book from 2009 *What Is Posthumanism?* (Wolfe, 2009: xiii–xviii). There seems to be a teleological trajectory, which transcends not only the humanist conceptualisation of the human but also the human itself, and it does so along the lines of the axiology animal-human-post-human-full automation. At one point in her argumentation as to why she embraces post-humanism in spite of the fact that it causes "deep concern for the status of the human" (Braidotti, 2013: 64), Braidotti states that the technologically enhanced post-humanism represents "an evolution" (2013: 64). Admittedly, she makes a trans-speciesist argument in favor of a vitalist concept of "life"; in favor of the body and the non-human (including the animal), she insists on a vitalist continuum and attacks capitalist commodification of life (Braidotti, 2013: 62–64). Nonetheless, further on and on the pages of the same chapter, its technological mutation as "advancement of evolution" is advocated too. I subscribe to Wolfe's generalisation that the majority of the post-humanists, in particular those of the "cyborg strand," end up sounding like transhumanists despite the utterly opposite and playfully ironic and ambivalent stance of Haraway's manifesto (Wolfe, 2009: xiii). Haraway's inhuman or the cyborg remains monstrous—it does not culminate in a unification of the two elements that, ultimately, "makes sense" (such as being an evolutionary step). At the heart of Haraway's inhuman, there is an element of inanity, or of the gaping real, that escapes meaning and philosophy (Haraway, 2016: 10–17).

The cyborg does not serve the "advancement of humanity" overcoming itself, making the next evolutionary step. In her later work, Haraway compares the inhuman to Cthulhu—it is closer to an animal than to the flat-surfaced intelligent and anthropomorphic Uebermensch of automated reason or the cosmology of artificial general intelligence (AGI) (Haraway, 2016). It is not a proposal that is anti-humanist as in anti-human: it could be seen as a radical deconstruction of the modern notion of the human and humanism arriving at a new definition of the "human"—a radical hybridity of the animal of *prosthesis*.

> Communications technologies and biotechnologies are the crucial tools recrafting our bodies. These tools embody and enforce new social relations for women worldwide. Technologies and scientific discourses can be partially understood as formalizations, i.e., as frozen moments, of the fluid social interactions constituting them, but they should also be viewed as instruments for enforcing meanings. The boundary is permeable between tool and myth, instrument and concept, historical systems of social relations and historical anatomies of possible bodies, including objects of knowledge. Indeed, myth and tool mutually constitute each other. (Haraway, 1991: 165)

The two elements, the animal and the prosthesis (or technology), are equally defining of the hybrid and neither is superior in relation to the other; the dyad is "radical" in Laruellian sense, which will be explained in the pages that follow. The two do not amount to a unifying single sense or, for that matter, to any sense. The inhuman is homologous to the non-philosophical non-human (O'Maoilearca, 2014: 113–129) or to Laruelle's human-in-human (1995) that is determined in the last instance by the real irreducible to language. The inanity of the inhuman, or of the non-human, is the gaping real at the heart of a selfhood; the post-structuralist turn has reduced to an effect of the signifying automaton, i.e., the subject. Pure physicality or materiality, regardless of whether living or not, synthetic or artificial, if devoid of signification assumes the status of the real—that which escapes language, meaning, sense, which is the unruly, the absurd, the *unheimlich* (uncanny and outlandish) out-there. In Laruellian sense, a dyad is radical insofar as its components are not determined by the relation of one of the elements to the other but rather by the real, inside the dyad and the real of the dyad itself as determining materiality. In other words, the relation between the two is unilateral.

The radical dyad and the method of dualysis

The presence of one of the elements is treated by the other as the real. Considering they do not amount to a meaning achieved through unification, they do not interact in order to produce a truth but are rather unilaterally exposed to one another; considering they serve as the delineation or exteriority to one another, their relation is unilateral. Such unilateral relation, when transformed into a method of non-philosophy, i.e., of a thought that seeks to correlate with the real while affirming its fundamental foreclosure, is what Laruelle calls the procedure of dualysis (Laruelle, 1989: 93–95). The relation of the two elements in Laruelle's human-in-human, namely of the real and the transcendental (or the instance of language), is unilateral and the dyad's constitution could be subjected but to a dualysis rather than analysis (Laruelle, 1995: 221–224). The relation between the real and language, thought and the real, the human-in-human insofar as the real and its subjectivity insofar as a formation of language is based on the same logic of unilaterality, which is the foundation of Laruelle's method of dualysis (Laruelle, 1989: 13–14 et passim). In Laruelle, the relationship between truth and the real has been radically shifted or has undergone a non-Euclidian transformation: the thought seeks to "describe" the real while admitting its radical foreclosure (Laruelle, 2014: 144, 161). Laruelle explains the concept of "truth"—it is the product of the philosophical desire to create a reality of transcendence of the real, or sublimation of the real into sense, meaning, intellect as perfected form of the real, as if a more evolved plane of realness (Laruelle, 1989: 54–58). The non-philosophical aspiration for knowledge approximates in ambition and in manner that of the sciences—it "describes," explains the workings of the real or the exteriority thought seeks to understand and "domesticate" (Löffler, 2018: 14–18) without the pretension to accomplish unity with it, a dialectical mutual transformation, sublimation, or elevation of any sort.

The real remains an ultimately messy exteriority and science submits to this fact. Such is science's metaphysical choice, I would say: even if it does not pose metaphysical questions, science has taken positions on a number of fundamental questions of metaphysical nature that define it as a form of intellectual production. For example, as Laruelle argues, science accepts thought's finitude and the real's foreclosure as the determination in the last instance of its practice (Laruelle, 2010b: 233). The real remains obstinately indifferent to the pretensions of language or thought whereas language continues to unilaterally correlate with the real seeking to mediate it (Laruelle, 1989: 56). By way of "dualysis," the non-philosophical posture of thought and language mediates its object of knowledge, i.e., philosophical transcendental material (Laruelle, 1989: 18–20 et passim), while submitting to the diktat of the real. It establishes *mimesis* of the posture of scientific thought while operating with the *chôra* of philosophical material (Laruelle, 1989: 64–69, 133). Or in Laruelle's own words:

> We are abandoning the traditional ambitions of philosophy—they are but hallucinations to us—and vindicating finitude, precisely the "radicality" or "finitude" of scientific posture. (Laruelle, 1989: 27)[1]

---

[1] My translation from the original French. All of the citations that refer to the original French publication from 1989 are mine. When a published English translation is referenced, it is the one released by Univocal Press in 2013 and translated by Taylor Adkins. In the subsequent chapters, I am referencing the translation more often than the original. In the Introduction, however, as I am presenting the fundamentals of the terminology I am choosing to refer to the original rather than the translation.

Laruelle's non-philosophical method is realist. Nonetheless the realism of non-philosophy is not indebted to a particular philosophical doctrine. It emulates the realism of Marx's writing. In *Introduction to Non-Marxism* (2014), Laruelle affirms Marx's project of exit from philosophy—by way of philosophical material—and the form of realism it brings forth. He expresses his reservations toward dialectical-materialism as profoundly philosophical but nonetheless admits that Marxism is the only successful project of establishing a non-philosophical science of humanity, next to that of psychoanalysis (Laruelle, 2014: 68).

> It is impossible, even in Freud and in Marx, and even more so in philosophy, to find the radical concepts of the Real and the universal—only those of the unconscious and productive forces, of desire and work. But after this discovery, psychoanalysis and Marxism take on more than a new meaning—a transformation of their theories into simple materials. Such disciplines demand more than a simple theoretical revision—a discovery of a "non-" that is an effect-(of the)-Real or its acting. Different from a philosophy, such theories demand that they not be relatively "forgotten," superseded, reactivated by and for another but transformed in a heteronomous way by this "non-" that is the effect of radical immanence. (Laruelle, 2014: 68)

Let us note that "dialectical-materialism" was not Marx's epistemological commitment or at least he never used those words to describe the tenets of his science (Wood, 2005: 212–213). Indeed, Marx's method is what we would call materialist, but he gave preference to the words "realist" and "naturalist" to describe it instead of "materialist": he did so in *Philosophical-Economic Manuscripts 1884* as well as in *Communist Manifesto*. Let us note in the following quote from *The Communist Manifesto* the discursive continuity between "the young and the older Marx" when it comes to the notions of the real and natural(ism), notwithstanding the surprisingly masculinist—I would not call them sexist as the *Manifesto* vehemently advocates full equality between men and women—and nationalist overtones:

> The French Socialist and Communist literature was thus completely emasculated. And, since it ceased in the hands of the German to express the struggle of one class with the other, he felt conscious of having overcome "French one-sidedness" and of representing, not true requirements, but the requirements of Truth; not the interests of the proletariat, but the interests of Human Nature, of Man in general, who belongs to no class, has no reality, who exists only in the misty realm of philosophical fantasy. (Marx and Engels, 1969b: 30)

In fact, Marx dedicated pages to the question of materialism—in particular, in his critique of Feuerbach—only to criticise the unavoidable residuals of philosophy in it. Instead, the science based on an exit from philosophy seeks to establish itself in the following way and with the following goal:

> Communism as the positive transcendence of private property as human self-estrangement, and therefore as the real appropriation of the human essence by and for man; communism therefore as the complete return of man to himself as a social (i.e., human) being—a return accomplished consciously and embracing the entire wealth of previous development. This communism, as fully developed naturalism, equals humanism, and as fully developed humanism equals naturalism; it is the genuine resolution of the conflict between man and nature and between man and man—the true resolution of the strife between existence and essence, between objectification and self-confirmation, between freedom and necessity, between the individual and the species. Communism is the riddle of history solved, and it knows itself to be this solution. (Marx, 1959: "Private Property and Communism")

Humanism is equated with naturalism and thereby a certain destabilisation of the anthropocentric worldview is introduced. The fact that "the human essence" is discussed and a vision of its realisation is proposed does not necessarily imply a form of philosophical humanism or anthropocentrism of any sort. The subject matter of study is the reality of "the species being of humanity" and the pursuit of its determination in the last instance. The determination is, in its last instance, the physicality of the "species being" of humanity or the aspects of "the real" and "the sensuous" underlying social relations. My research has shown that wherever one would expect for the term "materialism" or the material to appear in a writing by Marx, regardless of whether one of the young or the mature Marx, "the real," "the sensuous," and "the physical" are used instead. At places Marx is very explicit about the terminological choice at issue:

> The chief defect of all hitherto existing materialism—that of Feuerbach included—is that the thing, reality, sensuousness, is conceived only in the form of the object or of contemplation, but not as a sensuous human activity, practice, not subjectively. Hence, in contradistinction to materialism, the active side was developed abstractly by idealism—which, of course, does not know real, sensuous activity as such. (Marx, 1969a: "Theses on Feuerbach")

Concurring with Michel Henry (1983: 10), based on his exhaustive analysis of Marx's archives and careful examination of his opus, in addition to the one I have undertaken myself in a previously published book (Kolozova, 2015), I argue that there is no such thing as an "epistemological break," and the terminology in the sense thus described does not change in the works of the older Marx to reflect such presumed break. Certainly there are expressions such as "material products," "material production," or "material reality" but their referents are independent from the philosophical tension between materialism, idealism, and realism, on the one hand, and Marx's epistemic choice, on the other hand. Even when the occasional use of "material" and "materialistic" could be said to have an epistemic sense, it nonetheless most often appears with an explanation that refers it to the notions of real (production, experience, etc.) or the natural but also to realism. Here is an example of the nuancing in the use of these terms:

> However little our written histories up to this time notice the development of material production, which is the basis of all social life, and therefore of all real history, yet prehistoric times have been classified in accordance with the results, not of so-called historical, but of materialistic investigations. These periods have been divided, to correspond with the materials from which their implements and weapons were made, viz., into the stone, the bronze, and the iron ages. (Marx, 1978: 138, note 5)

The attack on Feuerbach's materialism and philosophy, such as in *Critique of Hegel's Philosophy in General*, is not something the older Marx has abandoned. Quite the contrary, in a letter to Engels he reaffirms that his lifelong project concerning scientific treatment of philosophy has never been abandoned and that his political economy should be seen as part of that very same project (Henry, 1983: 10). Let us notice that the notions of realism, the treatment of the real—physicality, practice, and the "real abstractions" such as social relations (Sohn-Rethel, 1978)—and the stance on exit while still operating with philosophical material or via philosophy are homologous to Laruelle's non-philosophical project. Let us call these tendencies of critical philosophy with the provisional name of post-philosophy. I will argue in the chapters that follow that we can indeed place psychoanalysis among them, as Laruelle insists in his *Introduction to Non-Marxism* (2014), but also include structuralism and, in particular, structuralist linguistics next to it. As said, according to Laruelle and also according to Marx, this is a stance that is also the axiomatic precondition and the identity in the last instance of science or of the sciences (Laruelle, 2013a/1989; 2014; 2016).

Just as the two elements of a binary in structuralist linguistics do not yield a dialectical resolution or any other form of unification, but are rather discrete constituents, so does the method of Laruellian dualysis enable a treatment of the radical dyad of physicality (and animality) and the signifying automaton (including technology) as determined in the last instance by the materiality of discrete duality. The radical dyad's "identity in the last instance" (Laruelle, 2016: 17–24) is determined by the concreteness of its constitution, namely by the materiality of the animal-machine—or of physicality-automaton—minimal structure of discrete elements. Our non-philosophical treatment of the human invites the use of the terms "non-human" and "inhuman." The radical dyad is the identity in the last instance of the non-human, homologous to Haraway's cyborg and the inhuman, and its determination in the last instance as belonging to the category of the real insofar as the real is instantiated as a specific form of materiality.

The "identity in the last instance" is a transcendental entity engendered by way of "cloning the real" (Laruelle, 1992; 2016). In order to avoid confusion with notions pertaining to empiricism, positivism, or philosophical realism of any sort, let us further elucidate the concept of "identity in the last instance" with the following quote from Laruelle:

> We can call "science" a knowledge that is unilaterally ordered to the real. The thought of Identity as the sole (real) cause is the simplest of all and the most minimal. The most rigorous, the one that reflects rather than expresses the real's structure with the least possible mediation and that emphasizes this structure as the cause of theoretical representations. The poorest because it rejects—although it exercises itself as a transcendence or a dimension of the theoretical—every foundation in a metaphysical or religious transcendence: in an autoposition. (Laruelle, 2016: 61–62)

In *Introduction to Non-Marxism* (2014), Laruelle explains the procedure of cloning as thought's following "the syntax of the real" and as being fundamentally "descriptive" (Laruelle, 2015: 109, 144), which can be understood as mimesis of the real's structure. The task of science as "describing the real," according to Laruelle's definition of it, is similar to

Wittgenstein's idea of scientific thought acting as "Maßstab of the structure of real" (*Tractatus*, 2.1512). The identity of the last instance, or the Maßstab of the real the non-human or the cyborg is, reflects a structure of radical duality consisting of the physical and the automaton of signification, and of the animal and the machine, as an asymmetric binary irreducible to a single underlying truth that would redeem the seeming senselessness of the odd pairing. The binary carries a kernel of non-sense issuing from the mere materiality of the unity without unification, of the absence of an answer to the question of what such unity amounts to. It is not a step in an evolution because we have always been cyborgs (Haraway, 1991: 178), and it is not reducible to either animality or technology, nor to their sublation or sublimation. There is no contradiction to be resolved as their unilateral (non-)relation cannot produce either coherence or contradiction. What remains there, at the heart of this discrepant, awkward mess of animal and machine establishing some form of continuity between its two components, inhabiting the same real and subjected to a single determination in the last instance, is a certain remainder that escapes sense. It also escapes any teleological purpose such as humanity transcending itself with the help of technology or humanity transcending its estrangement from nature by returning to it as its true essence. The hybrid of physicality and automation—that can manifest itself as a hybrid of animal and machine—is the identity in the last instance of humanity. This understanding of humanity is neither humanist nor anti-humanist; it is non-humanist. It goes beyond the humanist metaphysics of anthropocentrism. Non-humanism remains aligned with some of the goals of post-humanism but it is also profoundly different from it: the identity in the last instance it seeks to explain and the real it correlates with is that of humanity, albeit explaining it by means of non-humanism. The non-human is endowed with both synchrony and diachrony; it has a certain structural transhistoric sense, which is nonetheless always already subjected to historical transformation. It can be seen as a radical structure and explained by means of Saussure's structuralism simply because it is a binary without unification or a dialectical outcome; it is the minimal structure, which is utterly senseless unless integrated in a finite automaton of signification (in Lacanian sense).

The speculative machine of capital: Marx meets non-philosophy, feminism, and animal studies

There is an almost perfect analogy between philosophy and capitalism if subjected to both non-philosophical analysis and heuristics based on Marx's writings (leaving aside the subsequent tradition of Marxism). Laruelle's diagnosis of philosophy—radicalised to its identity in the last instance rather than generalised—is that it is the product of thought grounding itself as the real by way of subsuming or sublating the real insofar as thought's exteriority into a mixture of thought and the real (Laruelle, 1989; 2013a, passim). Such "mixture" par excellence, the founding concept of philosophy, is "the being" (Laruelle, 2013a: 1, 2, 7, 12 et passim). The "being" is not only a postulation but also—and even more so—installation of the real insofar as its substance is to be understood as a certain truth, a conflation of thought and the real while submitting the latter to the former. Philosophical truth is an elevated real, a "perfected" real, or a real more real than the real itself (Cf. Laruelle, 2016: 10). This is what the problem of "philosophical decision" in Laruelle comes down to, ruled by the "principle of sufficient philosophy" or PSP (Laruelle, 2013a: 12, 77, 99 ff). Marx's "critique of philosophy in general" (Marx, 1959; 1968; 1969b) concerns its auto-referentiality, the fact that it deals with itself even when purporting that it explains the physical or material exteriority—philosophical materialism is inverted idealism, writes Marx, precisely because it does not submit to the real insofar as "physical, sensuous, lived" and "practice" (Marx, 1968; 1969a). The inability to think in terms of a "third person's perspective" but rather subjectively is what keeps philosophy trapped in its pretentiousness to inaugurate reality, to decide what is real instead of ordering to it, instead of submitting to materiality and practice as its determining exteriority.

> A being which has no object outside itself is not an objective being. A being which is not itself an object for some third being has no being for its *object*; i.e., it is not objectively related. Its being is not objective. A non-objective being is a *non-being* [...] For this third object I am thus a *different reality* than itself; that is, I am *its* object. Thus, to suppose a being which is not the object of another being is to presuppose that *no* objective being exists. As soon as I have an object, this object has me for an object. But a *non-objective* being is an unreal, non-sensuous thing—a product of mere thought (i.e., of mere imagination)—an abstraction. To be *sensuous*, that is, to be really existing, means to be an object of sense, to be a *sensuous* object, to have sensuous objects outside oneself—objects of one's sensuousness. To be sensuous is to *suffer*. (Marx, 1959: "Critique of Hegel's Philosophy in General")

The post-Kantian, linguistic turn—and, thus, "post-metaphysical"—response would be that the real in itself is foreclosed to thought and therefore it cannot be its object of theorising. The post-structuralist radicalisation of the same position consists in the proposal to think only the linguistic constructions of our realities, the economies of our languages as power, while assigning the real in itself—or the Real understood in Lacanian sense as per the post-structuralist canon—to the domain of unthinkablity (Kolozova and Trajanoski, 2001: 76–77). And this is precisely what a philosophy—based on its underlying mythopoetic drives—desires: a knowledge that has engulfed the real, grasped it fully, and absorbed it without a remainder in order to sublimate the real into a reality of truth, in order to elevate the real into a more perfect form of existence, one whose core or essence is "meaning."

The fact that the pursuit of the real has been abandoned by the post-structuralists and thereby its incommensurability with thought affirmed does not mean that the old metaphysical mover of thought has been transcended. Quite the contrary, giving up on considerations of the real insofar as thought's radical exteriority speaks of the conviction that only if the form of "metaphysical" knowledge at stake were possible the pursuit of the "truth of the real" would make sense. Thus, the post-structuralists would admit its relevance for theory only if the totality of the real, its "essence," were graspable or only if it had essence. Indeed, Laruelle is right; nothing has changed in the old philosophico-metaphysical equation real = fiction except that has been replaced by fiction = real. Apparently, the positions have been swapped but the equation remains unchanged (Laruelle, 1989: 231).

The circularity in which post-structuralist philosophy remains trapped in—and, for that matter, the entire legacy of the linguistic turn too—is one defining philosophy rather than metaphysics. The principle of philosophical sufficiency as opposed to science's acceptance of its own finitude, as Laruelle would put it, marks the difference between philosophy and science. Assuming the posture of thought defining of sciences in the treatment of philosophy and for the purposes of explaining the reality of the "species being of humanity" (Marx, 1969a: Estranged Labour) is what serves, in both Laruelle and Marx, as the foundation for establishing a science of humanity. Moreover, let us note that sciences and philosophy make a different choice, take a different decision, vis-à-vis the questions of accessibility of the real and finitude of thought and knowledge.

Therefore, let us note that what the linguistic turn should have been in search of by trying to approach sciences and separate itself from philosophical atavism is, in fact, the exit from philosophy, not metaphysics. Metaphysical questions could be seen as clones of the experience that verges on the prelingual, stemming from that grounding bewilderment by the outsideness, by the real as the limitation to one's self-expansion but also as an invitation to join it, an experience that invites not only philosophy but also science and art. The experience can be treated scientifically insofar as it is consisted of materiality, insofar as it is the instance of the real preceding thought. It could also be treated philosophically or metaphysically, the latter being a form of philosophy. Let us reiterate, in order to exit the viscous circle of metaphysics, we should first exit philosophy. Metaphysical questions as objects of inquiry are nonetheless impossible to "exit" or abandon. Moreover, to do so would be unnecessary as they are the prime movers of all knowledge, including the scientific. They can also be seen as objects of a non-philosophical or post-philosophical science of humanity, treated as *chôra*, as disassembled set of concepts not constituting any philosophical doctrine in particular or a coherent theoretical unity of any sort (Laruelle, 1989: 17, 29–31, 127). They can come from philosophy as a discipline or more generally from the "world," a term Laruelle considers synonymous with philosophy—both are defined by the same grounding decision of what the real is, and both seek to establish an amphibology of the real and thought in the form of (philosophical) truth (Laruelle, 1989: 12, 23, 27–29, 34–36).

In the quote above, Marx argues that the non-objective being, the one that cannot postulate itself as an object for a third person, in addition to being unable to postulate objects of theorising, but is rather preoccupied with questions of its subjectivity, is an "unreal being." It is an abstraction rather than material reality or the real as "sensuousness" (Marx, 1968; 1959). What he problematises here, but also later in *Capital*, is the substitution of the abstraction with the real—the attempt at reification (turning abstractions into things, engaging in *Verdinglichung*) of social relations (Marx, 1978: Vol. 1). Relations are abstractions and as such they have their material or real determination. The fetishisation of value, on the other hand, through monetisation and commodification, constitutes the grounding gesture of capitalism. The concreteness of the physical product is transposed onto the plane of pure value, absorbed in the signifying chain of M-C-M, transformed into monetary worth, into an abstraction conflated with materiality. Whether use value or surplus value, what is fetishised as commodity is the abstraction, the value itself. Even the materiality of money is a fetishisation of "social relations," which, with the acceleration of exchange, becomes unnecessary.

> In simple circulation, C-M-C, the value of commodities attained at the most a form independent of their use-values, i.e., the form of money; but that same value now in the circulation M-C-M, or the circulation of capital, suddenly presents itself as an independent substance, endowed with a motion of its own, passing through a life-process of its own, in which money and commodities are mere forms which it assumes and casts off in turn. Nay, more: instead of simply representing the relations of commodities, it enters now, so to say, into private relations with itself. It differentiates itself as original value from itself as surplus-value; as the father differentiates himself from himself qua the son, yet both are one and of one age: for only by the surplus-value of £10 does the £100 originally advanced become capital, and so soon as this takes place, so soon as the son, and by the son, the father, is begotten, so soon does their difference vanish, and they again become one, £110. (Marx, *Capital*, Vol. I, Part 2, Chapter 4)

The spectrality of this sort of universe, its autopostulation and sufficiency, its unrealness is similar to that of philosophy Marx discusses in the previous quote. Both are unreal as both do not submit to the real as their determination in the last instance. In this sense, they both produce the amphibology characteristic of philosophy as explained by Laruelle. The constitution of both universes, that of philosophy and that of capitalism, is identical in its axiomatic postulation. From this perspective, it becomes almost tangibly evident why Laruelle equates the notions of the world and of philosophy (Laruelle, 2013a: 101–102, 106, 142, 144). The real and the physical are in both cases mere "material resource"—that which ought to be exploited in order to create value—for the self-sufficient universe of pure value to be constituted and sustained.

The material for the capitalist machine: Animals and humans that can be reduced to animality

The capitalist machine of value production, the instances of quantification and calculation of worth, enabled by the infrastructure of the multinational and national banking and state institutions, rely on the combustion of the world of real economy. Commodities are created not in order to satisfy the general population's needs, physical and "spiritual" (*geistige*, as Marx would put it), not for their use value. Their determination in the last instance is not the material use but rather their value (divided into use value and surplus value)—thus exchange must be maintained at an ever-greater speed. At a certain point what is being exchanged becomes completely dissociated from its alleged physical referent, such dissociated purely speculative entities are, for example, derivatives, bonds the "finance industry" operates with as its "material." The creation of a "bubble" was inevitable in the first decade of 2000s. What collapsed then was the universe of projected values and the monetary profit that would have been gained from such projections—the real economy, the material production that sustains the livelihood of humanity, was in fact uninvolved in any sense and affected only indirectly. The M-C-M automaton has the intrinsic tendency to accelerate and arrive at its homeostasis of M-M. The following passage from Marx explains in what way:

> A more rapid circulation of money takes place whenever a larger number of transactions are performed with the same amount of money. This may also take place under the same periods of capital reproduction as a result of changes in the technical facilities for the circulation of money. Furthermore, there may be an increase in the number of transactions in which money circulates without representing actual exchanges of commodities (marginal transactions on the stock-exchange, etc.). On

the other hand, some circulations of money may be entirely eliminated. (Marx, *Capital*, Vol. II, Chapter 17)

It is not that the self-sufficient universe of capital underestimates the physical in the sense of a living and killable body and its aspect of animality only but also physicality as materiality regardless whether living or mere non-living object—the treatment of real estate in the post-2007 crisis, that is, the irrelevance of use value of housing, is based on the same contempt for the "merely physical (object)" as that for the exploited underpaid labor. Such is the treatment of nature as resource too. That is why, I argue, capitalism is based on a metaphysical fallacy in its treatment of the real determined as material or by a material instance. Similarly, for philosophy, a stipulation and its crisis or, god forbid, a collapse of a theoretical framework seem more real and urgent than the crisis in the real, tangible political-economic world and the destruction pertaining to the Capitalocene (Haraway, 2015; 2016). In both cases, it is more about the contempt for the real and the "objective" (in the sense Marx referred to the notion, rather than in the positivist sense: see above) than for the body and the animal exclusively.

"The human" is a matter of recognition of an *embodiment* of an idea, that of humanity. As said at the beginning, it is an invention of modernity and Enlightenment as philosophy. The model embodiment of the idea is the white man as patriarch. The rest of humanity has always strived for recognition as human from a lower or bottom position on the axis of humanity or from the position of the excluded, just as women, slaves, and people of color were at the time of the birth of the anthropocentric philosophy, sciences, economy, of the "world" as we know it. One might say that struggle is still ongoing in most corners of the world, including the "developed" ones (note: "development" is not an unambiguous term). The intellectual era of humanism coincides with the rise of capitalism and industrialist society. The human abstraction as subject of embodiment or value that can be attributed to certain entities and the human that can also be transformed into the abstraction of labor—embodiment of estranged generality—are in correspondence. According to bourgeois reason, the human dignity of the worker is intact by this process, as the sense of the self, self-awareness, reflection—all of the individualist and auto-referential categories of subjectivity—is deemed independent from the body as embodiment.

All forms of humanity that can be easily dehumanised, rendered representationally closer to the animal than the human, are mere resource of labor—they are not even subjectivities, not workers; they are simply "labor" as materiality. Labor is to be dispensed with in the name of the creation of value. "Human resources" is just a form of resource as are the other "material resources" so the pure and maximal value can be accomplished. In order to do so, it is necessary to reduce or completely eliminate the notion of use value, to expand that of surplus value to the point of irrelevance of any distinction between the two. The complete expenditure of all animality, as part of the expenditure of all natural and unnatural physical resources, is the precondition of capitalism's ideality. If it were to accomplish its goal of idea triumphing materiality and nature, as per Hegel, a holocaust of all animals is required, human and those deprived of language. *Politics of the non-human is indispensable for a postcapitalist vision of society and its socialist response.*

It is, however, the ontology or the metaphysics of the body-machine hierarchy, of the hierarchy of physicality and automation, of matter and idea (or intellect) as stipulated by philosophy that sustains the logic of capitalism and the destruction it entails. Exploitation of "resources" for the sake of "value" is a formulation that will always come up with all sorts of "progressive" mutations, all of them under the guise of (post)human rights, unless its status of a grounding philosophical-political axiom remains unchallenged. What enables its unquestionability is precisely the philosophy of this world—or simply the World in Laruellian sense—sustained by philosophy as an academic discipline. It is apparent that the metaphysical choice cannot be avoided or dismissed: the metaphysical question cannot be evacuated either from political discussion or from the realm of scientific inquiry. After all, science is about a different (from that of philosophy) stance toward the metaphysical hierarchy in question: its ambition is to explain the outsideness, the reality as exteriority and material world, and it is premised on realism, which is a position in relation to a metaphysical question, that of "is the outside world knowable?" (Laruelle, 2016: 39).

Thus, instead of evacuating metaphysics from the discussion, the materialist and scientific post-philosophical treatment of the non-human—or the animal with or without the capacity of speech—would submit to the real as its determination in the last instance instead of the philosophical auto-referential circularity. Capitalism is indeed a quasi-physical realisation of a philosophically postulated universe, much in the vain of Hegel's idea conquering nature by way of its annihilation yielding its transformation into the "Idea in and for itself," into the self-realisation of the Absolute.

The method of dualysis described above, likened to the posture of thought determining scientific thinking, as already said, submits to the real it seeks to explain, or to instantiations of the real, rather than to concepts, theorems, and philosophemes. It certainly operates with the transcendental, and the *chôra* derived from various theorems and philosophemes is the material the non-philosophical or post-philosophical thought draws on but in the last instance submits to the determining real. The real is not substantialised, it is not some vague absolute, it is not an entity, or, in Aristotelian terms, it is not *ousia* but rather *tropos* (or *modus* in Latin). Reality has its aspects of transcendence and of immanence or of the real as the determination in the last instance manifesting itself to thought as defining limit, as the Aristotelian-Lacanian *tuché* interrupting the signifying automaton, as trauma to language as automaton. It is thus vis-à-vis this instance only that thought positions itself in terms of unilaterality, or, in other words, thought always already presupposes that there is no relation of reciprocity with the real. The indifference of the real is irrevocable and the scientific and post-philosophical posture of thought is premised on the affirmation of that indifference. In Laruelle, this posture of thought is sometimes called a Vision-in-One. In spite of its seemingly theological overtones, "the Vision-in-One" is quite the opposite—it mimics the scientific submission to the indifferent determination of the real pertaining to a particular reality it seeks to describe and explain. The operation with philosophical and theoretical materials, the conceptual bulk it draws on, does not deter the scientific stance from its defining submission to the singularity it seeks to render intelligible. In Laruelle's own words, unilaterality (or "the Vision-in-One") and the synonymity of philosophy and "the World" are described as follows:

> The One thus described is unthinkable from the speculative point of view alone; it challenges the speculative imagination itself as power of synthesis of contraries, as transcendental power of philosophical imagery. It reclaims a thought without image, for, in a sense, it is always absent, at least invisible within the horizon of the World or philosophy. But it is not because it is unimaginable, non-projectable into the element of transcendence, that it would be unthinkable or ineffable. The philosopher wants to fold the real onto his thought and decrees through idealism that the real does not exist if he cannot think it. Vision-in-One constrains us to do the opposite: fold our thought onto the real by modifying the concept in accordance with it; no longer to be able to be willful, decisionist, idealist, but to be necessarily naive, experimental, realist, and to modify our traditional practice of thought and language in accordance with this experience of the One-real that we cake as our transcendental guide. (*Philosophy and Non-philosophy*, 2013: 50)

In Laruelle, therefore, to think in terms of the one is to think in terms of the real, and such methodological stance vouches for the determination in the last instance of the radical dyad in question. To affirm the radical dyad of the non-human is to affirm its singularity insofar as the real determining its identity in the last instance. The two do not produce a third entity nor do they yield one but rather remain radically two constituting a singular identity in the last instance, which is a single clone of a single instance of the real. It is a procedure similar to Wittgenstein's thought acting as real's Maßstab mentioned above and to Marx's thought determined by practice and materiality understood as post-philosophical realism. By way of such method we shall attempt to explore the socialist, anti-capitalist potential of Haraway's figure of the cyborg arriving at its radicalisation under the name of the non-human. We shall unravel its logic of exploitation as underpinned in a defining way by the treatment of the animal and the human body in its aspect of animality.

But in order to explain the resilience to criticism of the logic of exploitation of animal(ity), we need to divulge and explicate the logic of exploitation *tout court*. The tautological phenomenon called "value" and its fetishisation enabled by the hierarchical incommensurability between thought and physicality constitute the "moral substance" of exploitation. The suffering in the name of a "greater good," which once used to be the dignity of human life and now the Good seems to be detached from any "physical support" floating as a sort of an "in itself" and "for itself" (a self-standing Absolute), is a metaphysical fundament that pervades the political economy and "civil society" (in Marx's sense) of our era, i.e., the logic of patriarchy, race, and the treatment of the animal. In order to make the structure of exploitative reason, and its speculative metaphysics, as unambiguously identifiable and as universally applicable to the world-philosophy of today, it is imperative that the categories of analysis are as formal as possible. That is why we begin by radicalisation of several concepts by way of arriving at two categories of the grounding binary of the following planes of reality: the post-human and/or the non-human, capitalism, patriarchy, and industry as the holocaust of the animal. The grounding binary is constituted of the physical and the automaton.

Overview of the chapters

The physical and the automaton, introducing the radical dyad of the non-human

By abandoning the principle of philosophical sufficiency in the analysis of the dialectics between thought and the real, following Laruelle and Marx, we arrive at the determination in the last instance of what philosophy calls the "human." In its last instance, viewed beyond what philosophy postulates, the radical dyad, consisting of a signifying automaton (language) and body, we shall call the non-human resembles Haraway's inhuman. It is a hybrid of the two categories that establishes a material continuity whereas on the transcendental level the two categories are in relation to unilaterality (or non-relation, relation that is in no sense determining). The expansion of the philosophically conceived dialectics of the two —whereby the transcendental utterly subjects and supplants the real insofar as material— is the metaphysical foundation for the emergence and instauration of universes of purportedly self-standing automata: subjectivity (transcending body), capitalism (transcending matter), patriarchy (transcending human animality or femaleness). These self-regulating automata purport to be self-sufficient whereas matter is of marginal philosophical relevance. Matter has economic sense by way of being invested in the creation of value. Without *investment* as its teleological purpose, matter is senseless. The notion of the non-human affirms the continuity between the prelingual (or the physical) and the automation of signification on the plane of the real and the material, while nonetheless relies on the postulate that the thought and the real are unilaterally positioned. The real is indifferent to thought's making sense (of it). The dialectics of the non-human enables a different metaphysical stance that would provide the foundation for a universe after capitalism, one based on the presupposition that value, sign, and abstraction are in the last instance determined by the real of human activity and materiality. The reverse logic sustains the axis of the *automata of patriarchy, capitalism, and philosophy* and its pretention to sufficiency accompanied by the contempt for matter as nothing more than expendable.

Formalism of materialist reason

The notion of the non-human enables a more productive operation with its two constitutive categories, the automation of signification, and the real (mainly referring to the physical). The categorical clarity, and moreover formalisation of the categories, is necessary for an exit from the anthropocentric mythologemes that spontaneously inhabit philosophical thought. The formalisation we propose establishes mimesis of the practice of formalisation we identify in Marx's political economy, but also in structuralist linguistics, anthropology, and psychoanalysis. The procedure in question can be summed up in Saussure's famous statement that his science of the language has moved from the concrete to the abstract, only to return to the concrete in order to subject it to scientific explication. We identify similarities between structuralist linguistics and Marx's materialist formalism on the one hand and Turing's formalism and treatment of abstraction (Cockshot, 2012) on the other hand. Having endorsed Laruelle's proposal to exit the principle of philosophical sufficiency by way of reversing logic of thought and real and their inter-conditioning, we apply the method of formalisation on matters that have been traditionally treated within the framework of philosophy (including critical theory). Thought's posture vis-à-vis the real emulates the procedure of superposition in quantum theory. We find homology between the treatment of the real in Laruelle and that in Wittgenstein. The procedure of Maßstab (Wittgenstein) is in structural symmetry with that of cloning (Laruelle). The universalism proffered by the combination of procedures proposed here enables feminist universalism beyond the differences of cis and trans, culture and other variables that are treated here as richness rather than points of division, unified by the structural laws of the material reality of women's position in the contemporary patriarchy.

Subjectivity as inherently philosophical entity and the third person's perspective

Marx subjects Feuerbach's materialism to an uncompromising critique because it fails to transcend the bounds of idealism, arriving at the conclusion that it is the inevitable result of any philosophy. Finally, he concludes that the problem of all philosophy lies in its auto-referentiality and inability to submit to practice. His diagnosis is almost identical to the one Laruelle elaborates as part of his critique of the principle of philosophical sufficiency. Marx identifies one structural constant in philosophy, which is the organisational principle of philosophical sufficiency—the subjective perspective. It morphs the outside reality to mirror human subjectivity. This is also the organising principle of another tautological universe, that of capitalism—it is centered on the human and of the form of the "Universal Egoist" (Marx). The science of the species being of humanity postulates all reality, including the subjective, as object of investigation and, therefore, the thought as objective. This type of objectivity is placed beyond the subject-object dialectics. Rather it assumes the third person's perspective and from such posture of thought produces its "philo-fiction" (Laruelle). In this way, Marx circumvents the fallacy of Kant's *noumenon*. Laruelle recognises the foreclosure of the real. Put in Laruellian or Lacanian parlance, the foreclosure of the real is admitted in its radicalness and impenetrability whereas the thinking subject succumbs to its structure by way of superposition. From such position the practice of thought becomes the work of "coding" the real, transposing it onto the plane of the transcendental or language, *tracing* its syntax through signification.

Homologies and asymmetries between the automata of capital and patriarchy

We engage in closer examination of Irigaray's proposal to look at the automaton of patriarchal value production, and the treatment of women as commodities, as following the same ontological model as the automaton of capital. Therefore, we will investigate the structural homologies and political-economic symmetries and asymmetries between the two automata expressed in the formulae M-C-M and P(hallus)-F-P(hallus). By way of operating with the two formalised categories of the non-human, namely the automaton and the physical, we are able to identify the structural correspondences between the two automata, which are always already subjectivised. We revisit Haraway's figure of the cyborg or the inhuman and its presupposition that it is not a proposal for a human perfection or a metaphor of a perfectly humanoid machine.

Haraway's cyborg is not a figure of perfection, it is not a perfectly humanoid machine, and it is not about flawless accuracy and potency. It is a figure of blurring boundaries, of pollution and monstrosity—the cyborg is an irredeemable hybrid of animal and the automation of signification. We revisit the theme of the fallacy of the animal-machine opposition as both are on the side of the material whereas what lies on the opposite side is automation. The cyborg or the inhuman (or the non-human) is also a feminist figure because it not only disrupts but ultimately demolishes the "marriage exchange" as the automaton of P-P'. The transformation of *oikos* is the precondition of the political-economic transformation toward a socialist *oikonomia*.

New political economy is possible only under the condition of abolishment of the metaphysics of animal-for-killing

In one of his lectures held at Cerisy in 1997, Derrida states that the gesture of destruction of animals or of the Animal is foundational of all philosophy: "The gesture seems to me to constitute philosophy as such, the philosopheme itself" (2002: 408). The radical dyad of the (non-)human is fully humanised by the unilateral action of the transcendental to engulf the real and erase the physical by transforming them into a purposeful form of existence, into a truth or the being. That is the foundational gesture of philosophy indeed. The same metaphysics is enacted in capital's treatment of the physical: it does not seek to accumulate "material wealth"; it seeks to accumulate fetishised value, pure value parading as if material or physical. (It's not about the performances of the car the capitalist drives but about what it represents.) Capitalist metaphysics is anti-materialist and it is so because of the disgust toward animality and the embarrassing similarity humans share with other animals. Humanity that has been dehumanised (or is included in the category of "Man by courtesy only," as Haraway puts it), such as all women (cis or trans, regardless), workers of color, and the *homines sacri* of all walks of life but mostly emigrants, must be exploited on the basis of its proximity to the animal. Haraway's remedy is to elevate the use of animal bodies in exchange of value production to the level of "laborers." The procedure she proposes is philosophical par excellence as it seeks to emulate the structure of man's subjectivisation as wage laborer. Labor is always wage labor, explains Marx, and the producer in patriarchy is always male, demonstrates Haraway. Animal is material (matter) invested in the production of value by way of its combustion, destruction that is enacted not for economic reasons only but also for metaphysical reasons, those of capitalism and capitalism-as-philosophy. Laruelle suggests we assign a different "use" to the animal (including the human animal). I suggest we emancipate *use* vis-à-vis *value*, and having demonstrated that the specular world of purportedly independent (from matter) automata is unsustainable, refute the metaphysical fallacy of capitalism and, thereby, conceive a different, non-capitalist organisation of social relations for the species being of humanity and its interaction with the environment.

1

The physical and the automaton, introducing the radical dyad of the non-human

The subject as philosophical amphibology and the necessity of full formalisation of the notions of automaton and the physical

The category "automaton" as used here does not refer to machines as automata but rather to the signifying automaton or language as automaton in several forms that are central to our analysis: value exchange system of capital, language as in natural languages but also as in computer program languages, and, finally, patriarchy as the exchange of phallic power by way of the currency/fetish of the woman and the feminine. Let us say we will be using the term in Lacanian sense subjected to a Laruellian or non-Euclidean angle of analysis. But also, let us note that Lacan's notion of the automaton can be identified in the last instance with Saussure's conceptualisation of signification that can, in turn, be reduced to a finite automaton based on Markov's principle of "grammar as finite source" (Chomsky, 1959: 137). The finite automation in the sense of computer languages is conceivable by virtue of structuralist or Saussurean linguistics, which has proven to be applicable and moreover indispensable in the creation of artificial or computer languages as finite automata or "grammars" in their own right (Chomsky, 1959: 137–167). Saussure's structuralist theory and scientific practice of phonetics are founded on the idea that arbitrariness or contingency is what links a phoneme and a meaning, as long as we agree to it as a rule. The way we signify reality is an artifice that comes down to mere "tracing" or "écriture" (Derrida, 1998) that marks the effects of the real or the workings of the outside, of the real as exteriority. The craft of signification, the art of "coding" what goes on in the physical reality in order to produce a message that is transmitted to the other members of the species being (of humanity), is what determines language, regardless of whether natural or computer program languages. Those arbitrary connections are fixed into socially established rules of exchange of meanings and, through that, values constituting the Saussurean convention.

The structuring of that convention as a signifying automaton operating through three registers—the symbolic, the imaginary, and the real—proposed by Lacan observes the main principles of Saussure's structuralism: arbitrariness, convention, diachrony, and synchrony. Although the fundament of the concept of the automaton we will operate with here lies in Saussure's linguistics, we will refer to Lacan's rendition of it as well. The Lacanian generalisation of the notion represents its full formalisation that can cut across several areas of study while submitting to various determinations in the last instance depending on the subject matter at hand. By the latter we refer to materiality or physicality as substance of the real we have in mind, and we are pointing out to this in order to eschew idealisation or a reified abstraction of the real insofar as modality (or an Aristotelian *tropos* or *modus*). The Lacanian automaton stands in opposition to the real, and the two constitute an asymmetrical binary. It is one of the fundamental binaries for a world (in Laruellian sense, i.e., world as philosophy) or a society (in Marx's sense) that ought to remain a radical dyad; i.e., the two do not amount to any resolution of their "contradiction" or unification that surpasses the asymmetry. They are asymmetrical in such radical sense that they do not even create a contradiction: indeed, as part of a radical dyad, their relation is one of unilaterality in Laruellian sense referring to the procedure of dualysis. A homologous opposition is that of culture and nature we find in structuralist anthropology. This opposition is also there to signify the incommensurable asymmetry or the non-relation of the two constituents of the binary: the one is the limit (or the real) to the other whereas the "meanings" do not interact, do not mix, and do not constitute either a dialectic or a contradiction (Lévi-Strauss, 1969).

The real and the physical (or nature) are both on the side of that which precedes or excludes language. The non-relation or the relation of unilaterality does not mean absence of the physical reality in the sense of interaction or effect: relation presupposes a form of subjectivity, imagines an agency that holds a position, or mimics a stance or "treatment" vis-à-vis the other constituent of a binary. To act as the limit to a phoneme, in Saussure's sense, entails interaction but without a relation: most of the phonemes are coupled with other phonemes based on some physical requirements like occlusion (through consonants) or phonetic opening (through vowels). Saussure does not open a discussion of what the "binarism" entails philosophically but rather engages into exhaustive description of the operations of the phonematic interaction as materiality. Even though biologically conditioned, the principle or its "regularity" is mechanical:

> To give an account of what takes place within groups, there should be a science of sound that would treat articulatory movements like algebraic equations: a binary combination implies a certain number of mechanical and acoustical elements that mutually condition each other; the variation

of one has a necessary and calculable repercussion on the others. In a phonational act, the one thing which has a universal character that places it above all the local differences of its phonemes is the *mechanical* regularity of the articulatory movements. (Saussure, 1959: 51)

Mechanicity just as automation can have either organically physiological or synthetically physical or non-living material support. Therefore, both categories, the physical and the automaton, should be formalised to the extent that their identities in the last instance remain unchanged regardless of the physical determinant. (The variables do not alter the identity in the last instance.) In this chapter we focus on the opposition between the real insofar as physicality and the automaton insofar as signification. The two take place on two different planes: the immanent and the transcendental respectively. Notwithstanding the question of continuity between the two planes, their difference is unilateral and so it shall be treated as radical. Signification works on the principle of discrete sequence, which does not exclude the possibility of some form of continuity between the immanent and the transcendental, or mutual conditioning between the physical and the automaton. The mutuality in question is, however, asymmetric or unilateral whereby the real or the prelingual instance, which is in this case radically identified as the physical, is indifferent to such continuity or mutual conditioning. The automaton proceeds in discrete fashion, as an endless circularity within a finite system. One of the phonemes or signs works as the real or the productive delimitation of the other. This dynamic offers a possibility for a new epistemology or is pregnant with a philosophical potential that can be submitted to a "non-Euclidean" shift, a notion Laruelle uses to explain his declination of philosophy as non-philosophy. In one of his earliest published articles Laruelle argues:

> This [Jakobson's] overly vague and abstract definition obliterates two problems that structuralism avoids posing.

a) The possibility or rather the reality and means of passage from one contrary to the other: this requires an associative capacity [puissance], a retention of one phoneme that is unlimited as a flux when the other phoneme (either in the paradigm, or in the syntagm) comes to determine or limit it. This limitlessness of the phoneme is nothing but phonesis, and this is precisely and solely what guarantees the coupling with the following phoneme; in this way, due to the immanent concept of association, the explanation is freed from the recourse to the mental fetish of "evocation".

b) The non-reciprocity of the coupling of phonemes. The reciprocity of passage or symmetry is valid only for production (instance from which structuralism selects its abstract conception of language [langue]). In production, there is an asymmetrical coupling in the following form: an unlimited phonesis is cut off or limited by a phoneme which, in turn, re-launches as unlimited phonesis, etc., so much so that phonesis always identifies with the break that "is" distinguished from it: unilateral or fractional identification and distinction. These are the two immediate sides of the phonetico-phonematic entity or of the fractional organ of language [langue], which is an object of a complexity superior to that of the phoneme alone and is produced by associative contiguity of "contraries". All structuralists, but also Jakobson, remain content with an abstract and imprecise phenomenology of the break under the aegis of distinctive "opposition". (Laruelle, 1978)[1]

The unilateral or "fractional distinction" corresponds with the "mechanical regularity" Saussure writes about. Not all structuralists "remain content with an abstract phenomenology": Saussure establishes the science of linguistics

---

[1] The original reference is Laruelle, F. "Pour une linguistique active (la notion de phonèse)," *Revue philosophique de la France et de l'étranger*, Vol. 168, Issue 4 (October–December 1978): 419–431. I have used here Taylor Adkins's translation published on the philosophical blog "Speculative Heresy."

and its structuralist method without any ambition to postulate either a phenomenology or a philosophy more generally, in perfect compatibility with his epistemic principle to move from the concrete to the abstract. That movement, however, serves to explain the concrete: the identity in the last instance of the ideal p is determined by the material or as the real P, which is always either $p>$ or $p<$ (Saussure, 1959: 53). The ideal "p" is an abstraction and as such an instrument in explaining p> and p<. Therefore, the abstraction of "p" is not reified, "embodied," materialised but quite the opposite—the imperfect real of p> and p< precedes and determines the ideal as identity in the last instance whereas the ideal p is never realised (Laruelle, 2016). The epistemic model Saussure develops can serve the "philosophical consequences" Laruelle suggests but Saussure's project never set such ambition for itself. The identity in the last instance of his subject of study remains the language: Saussure resists the philosophical spontaneity of ontologising his explication of the identity in the last instance of language by expanding it into an image of the universe posturing as the real. The older Laruelle or the non-standard philosophy would not invite Saussure to engage into "philosophisation" of phonetics but rather to submit to the identity in the last instance and the real that determines language as the automaton of signification. The non-philosophical conceptualisation of language consists in subjecting Lacan's automaton to a procedure of "philosophical impoverishment."

Linking Marx, Laruelle, Saussure, and Irigaray to arrive at a full formalisation of the categories of the real (as physical) and the automaton

If we are to exit philosophy as Marx advises us to do and so does the mature Laruelle as well, the model that begins with and is in the last instance submitted to the "concrete" (Saussure) or "the real" (Marx, Laruelle) contains the potential to serve as a sufficient paradigm for a scientific investigation when the primary conceptual material originates in philosophy. In other words, it can serve the non-philosophical study of human reality under the prefix of non- (viz. the non-human). Let us assume that non-philosophy can enable full formalisation of a category and a method: the path would be that of unilaterality whereby, while submitting to the material reality as determination in the last instance, thought, having affirmed the radical dyad with the real, pursues full abstraction. The latter is not a form of reality or of the real but quite the opposite, an operation pertaining to the transcendental, a formation of language or pure signification. As such it is always already determined by a physical or "mechanical" reality. Marx's political economy undertakes the same task of full formalisation of the signification of the concrete arriving at abstractions as operations of the transcendental, but also producing a novel metaphysical invention. Namely, Marx demonstrates that there are abstractions, such as social relations, that function as instances of the real *sui generis* due to the fact that they yield materiality or realisations. Sohn-Rethel called these abstractions real, which is not to be confused with fetishisation and/or reification (1978: 18). The "real abstractions" are in their substance abstractions but they produce effects of the real, which is not the same as substitution of the abstract with the material, but quite the opposite—the abstract is affirmed.

> The historical materialist stands in irreconcilable opposition to all traditional, theoretical philosophy. For this entire tradition it is an established fact that abstraction is the inherent activity and the exclusive privilege of thought; to speak of abstraction in any other sense is regarded as irresponsible, unless of course one uses the word merely metaphorically. But to acquiesce in this philosophical tradition would preclude the realisation of the postulate of historical materialism. If the formation of the consciousness, by the procedure of abstraction, is exclusively a matter for the consciousness itself, then a chasm opens up between the forms of

consciousness on the one side and its alleged determination in being on the other. The historical materialist would deny in theory the existence of this chasm, but in practice has no solution to offer, none at any rate that would bridge the chasm. (Sohn-Rethel, 1978: 18)

To understand social relations as real without reification, or without the fallacy of substituting their status of the real with materiality, is a metaphysical and methodological invention of Marx formulated as consequently and as purely abstractly as possible. In other words, it constitutes the kind of formalisation we are in search of here. Namely, it is not reducible to the subject matter of his analysis, i.e., the political economy, but is rather a "generalisation" (Laruelle) that is sufficiently formulaic to be applied to other identities in the last instance with different physical determinants. For example, the same economy of use value versus surplus value, and the material backdrop of fetishisation that enables it, can be found in the exchange of women or patriarchy, as explained by Irigaray.

The value of symbolic and imaginary productions is superimposed upon, and even substituted for, the value relations and corporal (re)production. In this new matrix of History, in which man begets man as his own likeness, wives, daughters, and sisters have value only in that they serve as the possibility of, and potential benefit in, relations among men. The use of and traffic in women subtend and uphold the reign of masculine hom(m)o-sexuality, even while they maintain that hom(m)o-sexuality in speculations, mirror games, identifications, and more or less rivalrous appropriations, which defer its real practice [...] Woman, as object of exchange, differs from woman as use value, in that one doesn't know how to take (hold of) her, for since "the value of commodities is the very opposite of the coarse materiality of their substance, not an atom of matter enters into its composition." (Irigaray, 1985b: 171)

Women are de-realised even as use value and what is exchanged in patriarchy is abstraction or the commodified femininity, which serves the multiplication of the surplus value or rather the pure value of masculinity. Just as the "C" in the M-C-M formula can be expunged as it is a mere relay for the endless repetition of the M-M automaton, so, to paraphrase Marx, because *not an atom of matter enters the composition* of woman as commodity, the material woman can be excluded from the equation P(hallus)-P(hallus). The less physicality in the pure value of femininity the more perfect the finite automaton of patriarchy. The fetishised femininity, as any form of commodity, is reified abstraction. The token of femininity is exchanged only in order for masculinity to engender itself. Masculinity (or the pure value of the Phallus), speculative reason, and rationalism are endowed with the same contempt for the physical, narcissistic circularity of thought and disgust for the woman outside the signifying automaton of fetishisation, as demonstrated in Irigaray's *Speculum of the Other Woman* (1985b). Since Plato's *Timaeus* to modernity, the Woman is reduced to *passivity, matter, animality* and as such to philosophical irrelevance. The "C" or the commodity both as reality, physicality, and as fetishised abstraction in Marx's equation can be dispensed with precisely because it presupposes some reality for the physical, some relevance for the real that is detached from the transcendental, devoid of meaning or truth or value. *Physicality is to be used up completely in order to be transformed into pure value.* The automaton of capital, or the tautological machine of pure value, becomes gradually independent from its physical support and thus not only money but also actual commodity becomes superfluous as is the case in the finance industry. Thus, the exchange continues according to the law of capital's self-acceleration issuing from the purity of the most logical of all creations of language, the tautology—so, it becomes M-M. Interestingly, Marx uses a metaphor referring to patriarchy to explain the principle of capitalist speculative reason as opposed to nature and thus ultimately untenable:

> In simple circulation, C-M-C, the value of commodities attained at the most a form independent of their use-values, i.e., the form of money; but that same value now in the circulation M-C-M, or the circulation of capital, suddenly presents itself as an independent substance, endowed with a motion of its own, passing through a life-process of its own, in which money and commodities are mere forms which it assumes and casts off in turn. Nay, more: instead of simply representing the relations of commodities, it enters now, so to say, into private relations with itself. It differentiates itself as original value from itself as surplus-value; as the father differentiates himself from himself qua the son, yet both are one and of one age: for only by the surplus-value of £10 does the £100 originally advanced become capital, and so soon as this takes place, so soon as the son, and by the son, the father, is begotten, so soon does their difference vanish, and they again become one. (Marx, *Capital*, Vol. I, Chapter 4)

The abstraction of the M-C-M formula, if not reified and transformed in philosophical amphibology, is the method of the scientific inquiry of the species being of humanity, applicable, as demonstrated, on its social reproduction and the dialectics of sexes or genders. By way of arriving at abstractions that are as self-standing as possible, one remains inside the signifying automaton and on the plane of the transcendental. It is a position, which is close to that of science and outside the self-enveloped universe of philosophy because it does not substitute fiction or signification for the real. Producing such amphibology, whereby sign/thought/truth is indistinguishable from the real and usurps its position by some kind of sublation, is the characteristic of philosophy, argues Laruelle (2013a: 10). Non-philosophy operates with the "transcendental material" of philosophy but without the amphibology in question: the real is irrevocably indifferent to the thought that seeks to signify/describe it (Laruelle, 2013a: 45). By way of *mimesis* of the workings of the real one arrives at its ever more exhaustive "description," a term Laruelle often chooses when explaining the purpose of cloning or of signification that divulges "the way the real works." Laruelle's "cloning of the real," as mentioned in the introductory chapter, comes down to submission to the "syntax of the real" or to a minimal transcendental that seeks to "describe the real" rather than become one with its essence (Laruelle, 2013a: 45; 2014: 48, 109, 141)— "the being" is the paradigmatic and founding concept of such "mixture" of truth and the real as the defining trait of philosophy (Laruelle, 2013a: 14, 34). The real is a status or mode of reality; it is not a reified entity and it is not an idea or a self-sufficient and self-standing concept as it must be determined by different and endless configurations of material reality. The clone is then determined by the real as matter, physicality, or abstraction that affects the thinking and/or the signifying automaton as an instance of the real, involving some materiality or material effectuation.

According to Lacan, the signifying chain is an automaton, and so is for Saussure. Both of them are structuralists and both of them are scientists covering subject matter that is conventionally considered philosophical. The young Laruelle criticises the structuralists and Saussure in particular for failing to develop the philosophical potential of phonetics suggesting its philosophical double under the name of *phonesis* (1978: 419–431). However, a non-philosophical treatment of the transcendental material of structuralist linguistics and psychoanalysis would be to radicalise the concepts by way of unilaterality determined by the real or the physical. By way of methodological procedure of "philosophical impoverishment" (Laruelle, 2014: 2), non-philosophy remains in submission to the effects of the real while pursuing further formalisation of the concept making it susceptible to communication or intersection with other sciences. This formalisation is fundamentally different from that of positivism or the formalisms influenced by philosophical principles and teleologies such as the idealisms of logico-mathematical formalism or that of the philosophical legacy of Marxism, argues Laruelle (2014: 179). He does not seek to reduce logic or mathematics to idealism and hence to the principle of sufficient philosophy (PSP) but rather points out to such tenets in both disciplines, just as he does in the case of Marxism. Non-Marxism is a project of remaining in fidelity to the scientific or the radical core of Marxism beyond the PSP—beyond the auto-referential postulation and grounding of the real by philosophy, whereby the real is cancelled in order to be instituted by thought, the real is "mixed" with thought in a gesture of "autofetishisation" (Laruelle, 2013a: 12). The non-philosophical and non-Marxist formalisation Laruelle proposes is modelled on the method of quantum theory, i.e., a model grounded in physics and physicality independent from representations or one in which representation is in radical unilaterality with the real.

> Non-Marxism defines itself as a special "formalism" upon the theoretical plane. Not in the sense critiqued abundantly by Marxism itself, but rather in the sense that quantum physics has introduced. We will call "formalism" a theory determined in-the-last-instance by the radical Real, being, strictly speaking, like a non-theory or an impossible theory [...] Formalism does not describe anything of the invisible Real, it is not in any way "realist" or even "idealist" or has none of these pretensions, it is the theoretical style that is adequate to the unthinkable and the unknowable, a form of theory made for what is radically invisible or imperceptible in the forms of representation, but it puts together and "calculates" the phenomena or symptoms. (Laruelle, 2014: 179)

"The forms or representations" referred to in the quote seem to belong to the commonsensical reason and to philosophy or the view shaped by the "World" in Laruellian sense. A homologous concept could be Sellars's "manifest image of reality" (1963: 5–40), i.e., a representation that has not been submitted to the real and to formalisation of language. A rigorous investigation into what determines the identity in the last instance of the real seeking to "calculate" its symptoms, conceptually recreating the structure of the real in its static and dynamic aspects, invites an ever-greater abstraction or formalisation of concepts. It does not deal with the "invisible" that could be finally "revealed in its visibility." The real can never be transformed, reduced, or even approximated to representation. The real can be cloned, "put together and calculated as symptom."

If the language is an automaton, the ever-greater formalisation of it is an ever-greater automation. Thus, the non-philosophical language of non-Marxism, the post-philosophical political economy of Marx, and the pleasure principle (language) of psychoanalysis are signifying automata marked with inherent incompleteness. The self is a radical dyad of physicality on the one hand, that can manifest itself through the symptoms such as pain and pleasure, and the signifying automaton on the other hand. Language and the subject as its effect belong to the category of the automaton. Unstoppable signification is the substance, form, and mode of the subject. The automation can be interrupted, ruptured, or cancelled by the intervention of the real in the form of *tuché*, an incident and accident that traumatises the pleasure principle of language.

The real appears as a symptom of a "pathology" in Lacan, as trauma, and remains foreclosed to signification; it is the symptom of signification failing. It is not merely physical even though always materialised and effectuated through the body, but it is indeed the real that can be the modus of an abstraction too or an effect of the transcendental. The automaton understood in this sense, as well as the real as *tuché*, is based on Lacan's psychoanalysis but it has an Aristotelian history (Lacan, 1998: 52). Such incident, disruption and failure of signification, is either caused by or results into a physical failure in other forms of automation, such as the digital and the value exchange system of capitalist economy. The crash of the self-sufficient universe of value production of finance economy results into the trauma of homelessness, poverty, and decreased productivity in the real economy. A failure of the signifying automaton of computer languages is unavoidable if a problem of hardware occurs, and it often results into one. (We are referring here to the act or the performance of signification, not to the effects of successful communication or communicable message. As soon as the process becomes closer to noise rather than making sense a thrust of the real has taken place.) The subject of the capitalist world-philosophy, the subject of psychoanalysis, the subject as the effect of language is the "self" of modernity (and its postmodern variants, including post-humanism). The self as automated signification is the only form of selfhood available to the post-structuralist world-philosophy. Subject/ivity is the self of capitalism or of capitalism as philosophy (and the other way around).

The non-human is affirmed by the materiality of the dyad and the interstice at its heart

The non-philosophical conceptualisation of the self, and I am expanding the category to include the other forms of theoretical-methodological exit from philosophy's sufficiency as its principle, thus also Marx, psychoanalysis, and linguistics, does not reduce the radical dyad of physicality/automaton to one of its constituents. It is determined by the radical dyad as its identity in the last instance and it is determined by the materiality or the real of the last instance. The real is that of the dyad, of its internal unilaterality and the interstice at the center of it. We have called this reality of selfhood the non-human: the interstice is insurmountable; the physical and the automaton are one under the identity in the last instance but a unification does not take place. At the heart of it there is something that escapes sense—it can be intellectually grasped, it can be "described" or cloned, a Wittgensteinian Maßstab could be produced of it, but it escapes reason and its human shape (philosophy). Just as any other reality explained by science, which "does not make sense" even when explained how it works because it does not reveal the purpose of its existence, it does not seem self-evident what the non-human is about, what is its "meaning," the reason of its existence does not appear to be self-evident. It is a certain out-there, as meaningless, as monstrous as the rest of the outsideness that hasn't been domesticated via philosophy (including mythology and religion) or its humanisation. Intelligibility does not betray purpose and intelligence does not necessarily entail an agency or a subjectivity that embodies it; it is present in the bacteria as much as it is in Bach, as Daniel Dennett writes (2017). In the non-human, the signifying automaton plays the role of an internal externality vis-à-vis the prelingual self, whereas, for the subject, as an effect of the signifying automaton, the physical and the real of the interstice and the dyad itself act as an indifferent externality. Finally, the non-human in its identity in the last instance faces proper externality in the form of nature and in the form of technological universe.

> But intelligence is neither reasonable nor sensible nor lived. It is time for philosophers to choose between carnal reasoning and "excarnate" intelligence [...] Against Reason, Sense, and Life, against the glorification of the human which underlies them, hyperspeculation must mobilise the non-individual, the impersonal, the void, the multiple, the insignificant, the real-nothing. (Brassier, 2009; 2005)[2]

By proposing to "excarnate" intelligence, Brassier is radicalising the dyad of physicality and the automaton (or signification). This proposition is to be taken as scientific consequentiality in arriving at the pure categories or the abstraction that works as identity in the last instance. Any "mixture" with carnality is underpinned by humanist myopia; it is an anthropomorphic mythology or an anthropocentric eschatology. Thus, if we are able to arrive at a category that is applicable to other areas in the same way, it is an indication that we have undertaken a full and successful (one that works) formalisation of a concept that originates in a natural language and its common sense or

---

[2] Ray Brassier "Liquidate Man Once and for All" (originally published in 2005 in French) *In/Appearance Blog* (November 2009), available at https://inappearance.wordpress.com/2009/11/03/liquidate-man-once-and-for-all/, accessed on April 28, 2018.

philosophical use. The automaton is signification and its forms are language (natural and digital), calculation, and other forms of information exchange or the exchange of its fetishisation in the form of "value": capital and patriarchy as exchange of women (Irigaray, 1985a). The unilaterally postulated categories of the automaton and the physical enable a more exact explication of the non-human or the inhuman as the identity in the last instance of the human.

If the human is always incarnate, its identity in the last instance (that of the radical dyad) accounts for the double reality and the interstice as materiality at the center of it. If the real makes itself present in the form of trauma, the very physicality that is never fully grasped by the automaton (or the subject) *is an intelligible reality as any other physical reality* that plays a role in the constitution of the non-human self. The practice of signification is material and it constitutes a continuity with the physical or, together with it, participates in a single identity. Comparing philosophy with cinema, Ó Maoilearca writes:

> Laruelle's rigor is his radical consistency of practice: hence, as this quotation declares, it is the identity of logic that is as much in play as any logic of identities, and taken together, they must thereby mutate (understanding the transcendental as a transvaluation). From this perspective, logic has its own objectile identity, but one that shifts and so is multiple. The identity between philosophy and cinema, for example, is material and Real, involving cuts as one example (there will be others). Rather than solely involving the classical logical relation of "A=A" [...], it is the Real identity of what Laruelle sometimes calls "force (of) vision" or what he later calls "idempotency." Idempotency in mathematics and computing is a feature of repeated operations that do not result into anything additional to their first implementation. (Ó Maoilearca, 2015: 118)

If the transcendence or the automaton is unilaterally related to the real as exteriority, it is also unilaterally related to the real of not only its own elusive physicality but also that of the interstice between the body and the automaton. The physical and the automaton are determined by the real drive to domesticate exteriority, not as determination in the last instance of the dyad they constitute but as another materiality of determining effect. It is one of the materialities or the instances of the real of a determining character. It moves the two constituents of the radical dyad toward a common goal and that goal presents itself to be metaphysical (Löffler, 2017).

Philosophy does not precede metaphysics but it is rather the other way around: science, art, and philosophy but also common sense all seek to appease the metaphysical anxiety at issue or, for that matter, any metaphysical question. The metaphysical question is in its last instance prelingual; it is consisted of an experience of fear, desire, and drive as reactions to a faced reality. Only in the second gesture is it transposed on the plane of the transcendental, cloned into signs, and transformed into a language and, therefore, a question. In order to arrive at the identity in the last instance of that question, one has to step out of philosophy's circularity and submit to the particular metaphysical reality as an instance of the real and materiality. Experience is in the last instance determined by physicality as passivity par excellence, even if the experience in question is one of speech or being a subject of signification, i.e., driven by intentionality, acting as agency. I argue that the philosophical humanisation of the hybrid whereby the phantasm of domestication assigns priority to its own domain, i.e., the transcendental, can be sustained only by gradual annihilation of the physical. Thus, the biological, the bodily of its own non-human self and of the exterior world, is reduced not only to resource of self-sustainability but also to material that through its dematerialisation becomes "pure value."

The transformation at issue can take the form of commodity, money, monetisation-transcending value, virtue, dignity, a "life worth living." Capitalism is, therefore, concerned not only with material wealth but with value as such and as an entity in itself and for itself. The destruction of physicality, insofar as brute materiality or animality that cannot be transformed in pure value or in purity of value because of too much residual of materiality, is the main concern of capitalism, its teleology, and theology. The transhumanist phantasm is of metaphysical nature, an aspiration to erase any trace of the embarrassing remainder of our own animality or of physicality *tout court*, as that "dumb" presence, embarrassing mess of organic and inorganic vulgarity insulting the nobility of pure transcendence. I agree with Cary Wolfe when he writes that all conceptualisation of post-humanism that attributes the role of an "evolutionary step" to technology—and of transcendence of humanity realised—is in its last instance transhumanism or fundamentally not different from it, and this is my paraphrase not a quote (Wolfe, 2009: xv–xvii).

The emancipation of materiality and physicality from the pretentiousness of the philosophical self, or from the humanist self (even when it calls itself post-humanist), is not only about political struggle against exploitation. It is indeed the dehumanised or animalised body that is most exploited and the brutality of exploitation depends on the level of dehumanisation and reduction to animality. Thus it is about a fallacy in the treatment of a metaphysical question consisting in a gesture of "philosophical spontaneity" to posit what counts as real and what is to be reduced to unrealness due to its worthlessness, whereby the real submits to the "true" rather than the other way around. *Workers without workers' rights and workers without the status of workers are hardly agencies of any sort—they are the flesh that should be exhausted in order to produce value as commodity and monetary value.* The production process is as automated as the logic of capitalism necessitates it to be regardless of the physicality of the workforce. Inside the automaton of fetishised value production, the workforce can be considered a resource, mere material, rather than agency of labor. Precisely because labor can be replaced by an activity of a machine—but is not when human labor is the cheaper workforce—it can be treated as investment in material resources and in that capacity only it plays part in the equation forming the price. Thus, it is the physical, the animal and nature, it is materiality of "use value" and the real production, that needs to be delivered from exploitation, not the "workers" only, especially because many of the global labor force are bereft of the status (of workers). And the need to do so is not only moral but also political in the sense of political economy: capitalism is based on a flawed phantasm that the universe of pure value is self-sufficient on sustainable basis, based on an abstracted materiality as endlessly mutable resource. A political economy detached from the material is untenable. If technology or simply machines are seen as means of production, instead of being humanised in order to obtain the status of subjectivities, which is the only discussion of politics the post-structuralists understand, they would have to be seized by the proletariat (those who are there to lend their abstracted labor for wage).

The physical and the consciousness of the exploited (rather than the proletariat)

The non-philosophical or the non-Marxist way to proceed toward a political overhaul, which will indeed be a simple outcome of an irreparable contradiction rather than a revolution, does not rely on the development of "class consciousness." Classes are strata in a society that humanises and subjectivises labor by way of fetishising it as profession according to a hierarchy of manual and intellectual labor, material and immaterial labor. They presuppose individuation according to a bourgeois dream of humanity, that involves reason, enlightenment, progress, and personal success. The dehumanised masses, the human animal reduced to resource, will act as an agency of revolt against the suffering but also against the senseless discrepancy between the production and absence of demand, and against the privatisation of what has proven to be sustainable in the form of commons (aspects of the internet, for example). Internet as a means of production is in the hands of the users but they do not have the ownership of it as private property, which is, as Marx explains, always the product of a legal act (*Capital*, Vol. III, Part 6). The users produce most of its contents and in a way they "own" it or rather have access to it but without the claim of private property. It is an indication that the means of production could be owned by the producers without owning them in the sense of private property as the result of a legal act. The claim of individuals to private ownership becomes senseless as the producers can always create and recreate richer, more vibrant, more exciting platforms of information exchange than those who have fenced off a domain and called it their own. Similar logic of cooperation, self-management, and productivity can be applied on material production or in the "real industry." The automaton of signification of use value—without a room for surplus value—based on creativity instead of destruction invites different treatment of all animals including the (non)human. In the last instance, its possibility is determined by the real of the revolt of the exploited and is, therefore, based on consciousness of the exploited (rather than "class consciousness")—and they are all dehumanised or never fully if at all humanised animals. The consciousness will be that of and against the exploited animal, body, nature, real economy, and reality in the name of projected values and virtues; it will be a common consciousness of those acting in the name of the "physical and spiritual wellbeing" (Marx, *Economic-Philosophic Manuscripts* 1844) sacrificed to projections, speculations, and valorisations.

Let us recall that Marx equates naturalism and humanism, but let us not forget that in doing so he undertakes decentering of the humanist perspective insofar as it is philosophically determined. The decentering does not take place only in *Capital* but also in the early works such as *Economic-Philosophic Manuscripts* 1844: the insisting that humanism equals naturalism is insisting on the materialist epistemic foundation, on the "real and sensuous" (as material/ist) and the "physical," notions Marx resorts to regularly in his entire opus, and in particular in the early works, in describing what has subsequently become matter and materialism in Marxist theoretical tradition.

The chief defect of all hitherto existing materialism—that of Feuerbach included—is that the thing, reality, sensuousness, is conceived only in the form of the object or of contemplation, but not as a sensuous human activity, practice, not subjectively. Hence, in contradistinction to materialism, the active side was developed abstractly by idealism—which, of course, does not know real, sensuous activity as such. (Marx, 1969a: *Theses on Feuerbach*)

The epistemological reversal Marx proposes relies on a metaphysical shift of perspective: it is the "sensuous" (physicality) that determines the real, or the real in its last instance is material (something that can be known through senses). The workings of the human mind, the interpretation of the outside reality, and the social relations as materially determined reality in their own right do not fashion reality but rather succumb to the real. The externalisation of human nature, the birth and life of *techné*, is in continuity with "nature" or with the laws of the physical out-there rather than in conflict with them as such would be the hallucinatory perspective of philosophy: a mental projection of reality pretending to supplant the real by way of acquiring recognition as such. The recognition in question takes place through the operations of signification: assigning value (monetarised or fethishised in a different form) to the mute real through a signifying automaton.

The radical dyad of the non-human is sustainable as such if neither the unstoppable chatter of the automaton subjects the physical part nor does the physicality prevail over language through some form of catatonia. The latter is possible, however, if the automaton fails to resume after an instance of *tuché* intervenes. The automaton, if detached or radically indifferent to the physical, is indifferent to its failure. The opposite is the prerequisite for a post-philosophical and scientific thought: the assumption that the real is indifferent to thought's aspirations or, simply, to the pretensions of the signifying automaton, as per the non-philosophical theory of the PSP. If signification collapses, a physicality that borders with the prelingual (if organic or living) or numb physicality utterly indifferent to the automaton and thought remains almost unaffected. We can call this state catatonic only because some forms of materiality can experience the physical state of deprivation from the transcendental or language. This is a dystopic phantasm—an irreversible collapse of signification as endless variety of automation is hardly imaginable, the physical has always been subject to human ruse (as *metis*)[3] and, therefore, exploitation. Vernant's materialist genealogy of the Ancient Greek common sense, religious and technological idea of *metis*, demonstrates that the subsequent philosophisations of the notion are based on the principle of philosophical sufficiency; i.e., they appear detached from the political practice out of which the Greek invention of *logos* emerged (Vernant, 1984).

The pretentiousness of intelligence vis-à-vis the physical, in the sense of presupposing its obsoleteness unless subjected to a demiurgic re-creation, has never been as pronounced as nowadays, at the end of the second decade of the twenty-first century. The automaton is believed to be self-sustainable, even if complemented with biological "material." In such case, the physical would not be a support of the automaton nor would it be one of the two constituents of a radical dyad but rather a tool in a utilitarian intervention. The dyad will be annihilated by reducing the physical to a mere resource for the only possible reality, that of the transcendental. The automaton of the idealist worldview, one that presumes intelligence is a self-sufficient form of reality habitually emulating morphologies of the human/ist world, acts as if it does not require material determination in the last instance. Thus the threat of a possible catatonic sinking would not move it as it does not recognise it. In short, for political, metaphysical, and scientific reasons, and not only for the sake of the moral axiom, the radical dyad ought to be recognised as what it is—a dyad

---

[3] See Jean Pierre Vernant's analysis of intelligence as a form of ruse or *metis*: Jean-Pierre Vernant, *Myth and Thought among the Greeks* (Cambridge, MA: MIT Press and Zone Books, 1983).

rather than a binary in which by way of hierarchisation one component is sublated by the other.

The moral axiom we are referring to is in fact a political axiom. Its determination in the last instance is not sentimentality; it does not re-act emotionally—it knows the exploitation results into destruction. It knows the world of "pure value" or value of purity to be dead and it refuses to be the material whose combustion sustains the Elysium of speculation and specularity. The prime mover of the revolt of the exploited and the real determining its axiom in the last instance is what Spinoza would call the *conatus*. The body seeks to sustain itself in life; the physical world of all shapes, or the "nature" as *chôra* rather than a unified form molded following the humanist assumptions of it, will endlessly strive to live and, as a consequence, reduce pain and increase pleasure (Spinoza *Ethics* III 29p, 30, 30p). According to Spinoza's concept of *conatus* pain decreases the presence of life whereas pleasure is life accomplished or perhaps accelerated.

> Pleasure in itself is not bad but good: contrariwise, pain in itself is bad. Proof.—Pleasure is emotion, whereby the body's power of activity is increased or helped; pain is emotion, whereby the body's power of activity is diminished or checked, therefore pleasure (III. xi. and note) in itself is good, &c. Q.E.D. (*Ethics* IV, 41)

The automaton, if not submitted to the material as its determination in the last instance, is deprived of a mover to sustain itself, to resume automation after overcoming the thrust of *tuché*. The category of the physical is indispensable to sustain the automation and it is its determination in the last instance because materiality or matter is the determination in the last instance. The real as modus can be of both material and transcendental origin, but, insofar as substance, it is in the last instance always material including the real abstractions (such as social relations, which are inevitably materialised). The self-sufficient universe of speculation or a self-sustained universe of the transcendental is equal to

Plato's mythology of the *eidon*. Materialism of the radical metaphysics of socialism is a prerequisite for communist social organisation (Kolozova, 2015). The tenability or the efficacy of such metaphysical posture of thought for an establishment of a communist system is supported by the fact that it produces an evident reason and an impetus for the exploited masses to seize the means of production. The detachment from the physical reality and the automaton's circular message about its own self-sufficiency, which is not relayed to the exploited bodies, "muscles, nerves and brains" (Marx, *Economic-Philosophic Manuscripts 1844*), exposes its employability, its use value, whereas the surplus value is irrelevant to the exploited considering they are excluded from the chain of exchange. Therefore, the use value, which is that of technology being a means of production, is what the exploited must seize in order to sustain themselves in life. The automaton, on the other hand, does not care about life and its unstoppable circularity is not moved by anything that would remotely resemble a "desire" to stay "in life." It is indifferent to the possibility of its own failure.

The question of "the rights of the animals" can fall into the trap of a legalist aporia only because they are being conceived in terms of humanist individual liberties—the competence of language, subjectivation, and identification (identity) are preconditions for recognition. The claim to be recognised and the capacity of recognition are the indispensable elements of the concept of rights at issue, the only available in our era of post-structuralist *doxa*. They are by definition discursive, and linguistic competence is required. As Cary Wolfe notes (2013: 18–19), Judith Butler has made a step forward in the direction of transcending the mentioned aporia only to find herself falling back into it: in *Precarious Life* (2006) she argues for endless expansion of discursive intelligibility as the fundament of a limitless expansion of human rights or recognition of humanity (insofar as "grievable life"), immediately after having discussed the political relevance of the mere exposure to violence of the infant bodies and their innate vulnerability. Instead of radicalising the question of human and political rights by bringing it to its prediscursive origin, Butler proposes an ever-growing linguistic domain of intelligibility and recognition without noticing that it presupposes a center (of recognition) and an arbiter. The infants, the speechless and the demented, the animals remain outside the universe that is protected from violence and exploitation by virtue of its "inhabitants" being endowed with the faculty of speech.

> So when we say that every infant is surely vulnerable, that is clearly true; but it is true, in part, precisely because our utterance enacts the very recognition of vulnerability and so shows the importance of recognition itself [...] This framework, by which norms of recognition are essential to the constitution of vulnerability as a precondition of the "human," is important precisely for this reason, namely, that we need and want those norms to be in place, that we struggle for their establishment, and that we value their continuing and expanded operation. (Butler, 2006: 43)

This via proxy recognition is auto-referential and is awarded to the infant based on the projection of the linguistically competent human subject the infant is expected to become one day too, just like him, just like the human arbiter mirroring himself in the infant. But because "being human too" implies a subject of language and recognition, the awarded right may be annulled if the subject turns out to be unable to enter the field of language. Looking at Butler's proposal from a post-humanist perspective that exposes the historical character and the transience of the notion of humanity, and, therefore, of linguistic competence too, one recognises the limitations of the purely linguistic concept of the self (called "the subject") and the political. The linguistic concept of the political remains individualistic, presupposes an autonomous selfhood endowed with Kantian ambitions and methods of morality. In spite of its ambitions, post-structuralism has remained post-Kantianism and, therefore, its post-humanist vision too. The self that precedes language or remains incompetent in language, in particular the language in which one is able to claim one's rights, the beings that are closer to animals than humans (according to the arbiters of rights and recognition), should seek their liberation elsewhere—in the revolt of the exploited and its physical determinant. It precedes language, it can also incorporate language without being reduced to it, and it requires the overcoming of capitalism as the latter is defined precisely by the tendency toward a holocaust of the animals and all physical.

However, it is not the task of the individual self to liberate itself from subjection and exploitation. Capitalism is a metaphysical and political-economic formation that organises "the species being of humanity" undergirding social relations. In that universe, the phenomenon of use devoid of (use) value is on the side on the real, on the site of the mute and meaningless real. Therefore, it is killable, usable by way of its destruction. It acquires sense by assuming value or ascending to the status of "use value." The use value of the animals, human and non-human, in capitalist production serves the creation of surplus value or pure value, independent from materiality. The operation of transforming use into use value as part of the exchange value (split into use/surplus value) ought to be cancelled in order to cancel the exploitation of animals, human, "half-human" (or dehumanised), and non-human, as combustive material for the engine of capital. Such operation requires an overhaul of the entire metaphysical and political-economic system in place and is an objective operation, the work of a particular social *techné*, not an expression of subjective moral repositioning.

2

Formalism of materialist reason

Materiality of formalism

Marx's study of the species being of humanity institutes itself as a science that deals with value production and the relation of value to material reality. This is obviously a metaphysical question, but the suggested approach is scientific. Therefore, the science to be established in line with Marx's precept ought to operate with "philosophical material" but in a non-philosophical way. Laruelle has furnished a rich conceptual apparatus (at once lexicological and methodological) to make this type of science possible. The post-philosophical or non-philosophical Marxian approach I suggest here consists in the complete formalisation of the question and the language to pursue this science. This kind of approach should treat the material at hand—the conceptual material originating in philosophy—as material and as matter, if you will, along the vector "from the concrete to the abstract" (Saussure, 1959: 51). A similar trajectory is undertaken in Marx's *Capital* in which an exact understanding of "the concrete," the description of empirical data and the explication of its patterns, leads to discoveries about the laws that govern the exchange of goods or the market more generally and, ultimately, to the abstractions of "commodity" and "value." The examination and problematisation of the relation between the material and the abstract, between use value and exchange value, nonetheless requires the mobilisation of "philosophical material."

The problem of the tautology of value reproducing value, the detachment of the automaton of the market from physical reality, is a metaphysical question, and as such it should be radicalised—treated as material or real or, if you will, as a real abstraction, following Marx's model as further developed by Sohn-Rethel (1978). Instead of discounting metaphysics, one could formalise the language of inquiry while abandoning the principle of philosophical circularity or self-sufficiency. Formalisation does not necessarily imply computing or a closed automaton. Just like structuralism and Marxism, the prospective formal languages of post-philosophy, relying on the methodological model provided by Laruelle's non-philosophy, allow for poesy while being scientifically rigorous. This is due to the fact that they permit and acknowledge the remainder that escapes signification.

Having commenced with the concrete, computer languages go from the abstract to the concrete but also from the complex to the simple: this is a form of signification, and its erroneous fetishisation as a product of mathematics leads to a strange mystification of its operation—it is perceived as the product of "pure rationality." "Pure rationality" is a philosophical fetish par excellence for two reasons: first, a physiologically determined cognitive and psychical reality is transformed into a self-sufficient transcendental quasi-"entity," an ontologised agency pursuing a goal moved by the *causa finalis* of its own self-realisation in the form of an intelligent and rational universe, whereby an equation between what is real and what is true is established; second, a method of enquiry is ontologised and transformed into a substance (one that is superior to all substances), and thus the boundary that separated but also connected theology and philosophy is reestablished and reaffirmed. The reign of pure reason is structurally identical to the reign of the monotheistic god. Computer science is neither reducible to mathematical reason, nor is the latter reducible to the philosophical understanding of reason as pure and as an eschatological goal. Computer science and the tasks of automated signification are both linked to and determined by the physical support that conditions them as the constitutive limit or the real. Phonology is determined, delineated, limited, and scaffolded by physical phonetic possibilities just as much as computing is by its physical support. The division of the two categories and the dyad they establish is radical in and for the domain of transcendence (for thought), but this does not mean that their realities are unattached. Looking at the hybrid they establish in realist (or materialist) terms, the automaton is in the last instance determined by the syntactic possibilities of the real or the physical that executes the data processing. Deleuze and Guattari rightly pointed out that "abstract machines" are in fact material or that materiality itself is the precondition and the reality of signifying automata:

> The abstract machine in itself is destratified, deterritorialized; it has no form of its own and much less substance, and it makes no distinction within itself between content and expression, even though outside itself it presides over that distinction and distributes it in strata, domains, territories. An abstract machine in itself is not physical or corporeal, any more than it is semiotic; it is diagrammatic (it knows nothing of the distinction between the artificial and the natural either). It operates by matter, not by substance; by function, not by form. Substances and forms are of expression "or" content. But functions are not yet "semiotically" formed, and matters are not yet "physically" formed. The abstract machine is pure Matter-Function—a diagram independent of the forms and substances, expressions and contents it will distribute. (Deleuze and Guattari, 1987: 141)

Natural languages and other "real abstractions" (Sohn-Rethel), such as the value exchange system of money and commodity or the exchange of women (patriarchy), but also computer languages, are rooted in the real or the "physical" (Marx). Yet again, they constitute a radical dyad insofar as they are not amphibologically substituted or dialectically unified in a mutual way. In terms of structuralist linguistics, the automaton and the real relate to one another as the signifier to a signifier, whereby the one (signifier) represents outsideness and the real to the other. The automaton is never independent from and transcendent to materiality, since it is essentially materiality itself; consequently, it precedes "forms and substances"—it is "pure Matter-Function."

The automaton or pure form of language is not a form of pure reason and is in fact not a form of reason at all—it is as "absurd," or as arbitrary and contingent, as any language (in the structuralist sense): mathematical procedures are hardly present; it operates with four simple forms of calculation to signify everything. The mathematisation of data processing accelerates signification, which, in itself, remains as primitive what we find in natural languages and the other forms of finite automata of real abstraction (and some of its forms have been mentioned above): in computing, signification moves by very simple steps, step by step only very fast, to paraphrase Peter Dunn (Abelson and Sussman, 1996). It is indeed pure form, but the form is a mere convention that arises from the conditioning necessity of the material and is bound by its limitations, e.g., the physical properties of processors. In other words, the pure form in the case of the formalism of automated signification is not an image of "the truth of being" or a "reflection of the real" (in the form of a philosophical truth of it) but very much the result of syntactic possibilities conditioned by the physical reality or the materiality of the machine.

Technology as language

Language is technology, and technology is *techné*, not *philosophia*: *techné* exacts operations over and through the physical, not in order to "transcend it" but rather to use it in ways that help weighed-down animals, including human animals, in the physical reality they inhabit. Acceleration or flight is not concerned with transcending the physical but rather with its greater fullness and the exhaustion of materiality through expression. The signifying chain without agency—like any signifying automaton—is indifferent to goals like "the rule of reason" and "transcendence of physicality," including the philosophico-theological hierarchies they may establish. The motivation or the agency that propels signification and accelerates movement through physical space, or through physicality *tout court*, comes from the physical itself or rather the real of the "human-in-human" (Laruelle, 1995). The latter is the term Laruelle and non-philosophers use to refer to human identity in the last instance or to its status and state of the real—it is an instance that precedes yet prefigures language insofar as its identity in the last instance is determined as "human" (Laruelle, 1995). The non-philosophical concept of the human, however, has nothing to do with the humanist notion and project of the human as inherently philosophical. It is closer to the post-humanist idea or Marx's idea of the human as a social and physical being, an animal of pronounced and determinate sociality—the species being of humanity.

The agency of *techné* is therefore the non-human or the radical hybrid of physicality and of the automaton (of signification) moved by the needs of its species being. The agency of philosophy dreams of a fully autonomous signifying circuit or full automation or, in other words, absolute automation as transcending the real and the physical, a philosophical fetish.

> The machine tends toward autonomy and wants to think like philosophy does by making a success of its tour de force; it pushes autonomy as far away as possible and stumbles on the machine's agent manufacturer, but gets nearer to non-philosophy in so far as it has a presupposed. The idealistic argument according to which machines can build other machines does not, despite appearances, forget that a first constructor, an anthropomorphic inventor of the first machine, is necessary, but it can always hope to reduce this inventor in turn to a component inseparable from a continuous "man-

machine system," obviously at the risk of inciting protests from the rival party of Consciousness. (Laruelle, 2013b)

Non-philosophy proposes a concept of the non-human as the radical human, an idea close or supplementable to Marx's notion of the species being of humanity, which treats the automaton of signification as a reality distinct from that of the subject and the self and as one which determines "techno-logical" reason.

It is necessary to distinguish between an absolute commencement (thus relative-absolute) of the man-machine circuit that disappears in the system. And a radical commencement, a first techno-logy or a non-technology, a human subject in-the-last-identity but existing in accordance with variables that are technical discoveries: therefore, a human subjectivity but co-determined by the forms and the style of various technologies. This argument is apparently too simple and formal, but here there is also an antithetic of technology between those who want a first anthropological commencement of the tool circuit, a human agent, and those who, like Leibniz, infinitely prolong the circuit up to a God-machine or a universe-machine. Non-philosophy resolves this antithetic between the constructor man of consciousness and the machine of machines, by suggesting that its sense is purely apparent, indeed hallucinatory, and by relating it unilaterally to Man-without-machine, who determines a machine-thought qua clone of the techno-logical blending. This is to say that the hypotheses on the machine's exact origin and power remain those of the metaphysical order, and thus their solution is not within our scope. (Laruelle, 2013b)

Let us take a moment to explain the concept of "the clone" Laruelle refers to here, as well as that of the identity in the last instance, since their meanings are inherently linked. It is most clearly described and explained—or rather its use is best demonstrated—in *Introduction to Non-Marxism* (2014). The concept of cloning is inherently linked to the practice of "description": having admitted the constitutive foreclosure of the real, the thinking subject—or in Laruellian terms, "thought"—seeks to "describe" the real or the "syntax of the real" (Laruelle, 2014: 109). Procedurally, the following would be an operation of cloning according to Laruelle: by way of recourse to "transcendental material," or concepts as signifiers (meaning: parts of language rather than a doctrine) taken from the disassembled *chôra* of philosophical systems, thought mimics the real, which already has a certain "structure," as Wittgenstein would put it in his *Tractatus Logico-Philosophicus* (2.033, 2.15, 3.3442, ff). Laruelle does not refer to the notion of structure, nor does he explain more specifically the concept of the "syntax of the real." Yet again, we can safely claim that the notion of "syntax" can refer only to a structure of signification, which implies that the events of the real, the occurrences of materiality, or the processes taking place in constitutive exteriority possess a "structure" that can be signified. It is cloned as syntax similar to the way a sign produces a syntax in natural languages and is inherently endowed with rules of structuralisation. The identity in the last instance is a "radical concept"—rid of auto-referential layers of philosophy—that is affected by "immanence" (Laruelle, 2013b: 25, 26, 25, 30, ff) or is determined by the effects of the real, and it is in fact a clone and the minimal transcendental form of determination in the last instance. In short, identity in the last instance is still a concept and thus of the transcendental realm, but it is also a "clone" of a real, regardless of whether of an entity or a process of real abstraction or simply of the real (normally determined in the last instance by the physical). In Laruelle's *Theory of Identities* ([1992], 2016), we find out that identity in the last instance is indeed a clone: albeit of a greater transcendental complexity, it nonetheless departs from or is often reducible to a "clone" (the "clone" refers more to the procedure and posture of thought, whereas "identity in the last instance" is the outcome): it consists of transcendental material, of "theorico-technico-experimental ingredients" constituting the "real object" of inquiry, which is no different from the real (Laruelle, 1995: 92–93). Both the real and the real object of study contain "the same representations" but are of different status (and not merely epistemologically)—one is transcendental and the other is immanent (Laruelle, 1995: 93). For this reason, it is acceptable, as it often happens, that determination in the last instance, identity in the last instance, and the clone are terms used interchangeably. Let us note that the real (the immanent) and the real object (the transcendental) share "the same representation," which resembles Wittgenstein's thesis about the real and "the image of the real" (*das Bild*) sharing the same structure or rather his thesis that the image must be an image of the real's structure (this is explained in more detail and referenced below).

Computing, signification, and the philosophical questions of "intelligence" and "consciousness"

Nowadays, we speak of learning machines and of artificial intelligence, and everyone finds a way of participating in these discussions: scientists, politicians, philosophers, and the media. The question of intelligence has not only been treated by philosophy (and usually this has been done in the guise of discussions on "consciousness") but also by cognitive science, including psychology, neurology, and biology. Obviously, this is a complex question we cannot provide an exhaustive response here. However, we can move the discussion forward less ambitiously by revisiting Alan Turing's definition of computing as the single defining task of computers:

> The class of problems capable of solution by the machine [the ACE] can be defined fairly specifically. They are [a subset of] those problems which can be solved by human clerical labor, working to fixed rules, and without understanding. (Turing, 1986: 38–39)

By "understanding," he refers not only to what philosophers would call "consciousness" and self-reflexivity but also to understanding the rules of logical reasoning. There are no syllogisms, no logical operations, unless they are submitted in the form of algorithmic inputs executed as clerical tasks. Turing's machine can learn indefinitely, but the definition in the last instance of the acquired knowledge will still be "computing without understanding." In their book *Computation and Its Limits*, Cockshott, Mackenzie, and Michaelson explain:

> Mechanical procedures, also known as *algorithms* or *effective procedures*, consist of sets of rules that return definitive results after a finite number of applications […] Many mathematicians concentrated on trying to find rules to underpin "procedures," without reference to the "mechanical" application. In contrast, the British mathematician Alan Turing took the "mechanical" aspect as his primary focus, and elaborated the foundational idea of what are now called *Turing Machines* (TMs). (Cockshott et al., 2015: 68)

Whereas philosophers invest expectations of transcending nature through pure reason, of transcending the messiness of the flesh through the purity of intelligence (insofar as the latter is conceived as an entity with no human agency or as a quasi-agency with the status of an absolute), those involved in computer science have less pretentious views of their projects and the nature of their limits (or their limitlessness, for that matter).

Computer science and theory teach us that computing has very little to do with the science of logic, if anything at all, and that it only makes use of fairly rudimentary mathematical operations (Abelson and Sussman, 1996: Chapter 1). Computing is about inventing new languages of transmitting or mediating data, whereas the transmission of data, or simply communication, serves a social function. Thus, the processing of data, similar to the processing by natural languages of phonetic signs structured morphologically and syntactically, serves to exchange signs mediating knowledge, which has originated in some form of *experience*. The choice of signs as well as the syntax is arbitrary in natural languages and in the other forms of signifying automata. Yet digital automata are far more accurate and faster than natural ones—including those of social relations, such as capital and patriarchy as value exchange systems—thanks to the algorithms of mathematical knowledge and computing aided by calculus.

As already noted, mathematical operations are always reduced to the most rudimentary ones, i.e., addition, subtraction, multiplication, and division. As Saussure would say, the trajectory of computing goes from the concrete to the abstract and back to the concrete: all complex operations must be transformed into the simplest ones as conditioned by that physical instance, the processor. This is the case because computing is the *techné* of coding or cloning the real—being as successful in "describing" the real as an effect of a certain syntax as possible—rather than a form of consciousness or, for that matter, intelligence.

What intelligence or consciousness consists in, on the other hand, is still the subject of study in cognitive science. When posing the question of consciousness and self-reflexivity, both the sciences and philosophy contain a remainder that escapes knowledge and explanation, and furthermore, in its identity in the last instance, it is metaphysical. The questions of metaphysics shared by cognitive science, technology, and philosophy should be addressed at their radical core—that of metaphysics-without-philosophy or philosophy rid of "the principle of sufficiency." What is consciousness and to what extent is it constitutive of selfhood? What is selfhood, and can there be knowledge or intelligence without a sense of self, without the structure of selfhood or subjectivity and without an agency? In addition, are agency and selfhood to be equated? However, before addressing some of these questions, let us return to the practice of science and its language or procedures of signification. As already argued and partly elaborated, they consist of proceedings of ever-greater formalisation and ever-greater abstraction that have departed from the concrete or the material in a vaulted trajectory of abstraction aiming to return to the concrete by way of providing a structural explanation of it.

Feelings are irrelevant when it comes to the machine's understanding in the way Turing raised the point. If we imagine biological supplements enabling feelings or sensations in an AI automaton, they do not guarantee in any way that "understanding" will be enacted, mathematical and logical reasoning will be employed, or other forms of understanding will occur that involve the meta-positioning of thought, self-reflection, or the usage of syllogisms that involves no "statistical use" (as per the Bayesian method). Intentionality may be enabled by biological supplementation, but this alone cannot provide any guarantee that the automaton will enact understanding beyond mere computing. Perhaps we must address the question of subjectivity or, rather, selfhood and agency.

Formal language is the foundation of computerised signifying automata. Consciousness, selfhood, and awareness, on the other hand, seem to be inextricably linked with innovation or invention. Invention and innovation can be reduced to the procedure of formalisation, even though they are materially conditioned by it. However, the identity in the last instance (of invention) is determined by the transcendental-material reality of selfhood. We can also call it a subjectivity or an agency, but not a subject, which is a notion we understand in line with the structuralist tradition. Both of the former are terms determined in the last instance by the real of the non-human and its radical hybridity. Radical subjectivity is required to produce innovation: to be moved by a desire to explain outsideness, to not only understand the workings and the invisible laws of realities but also to control them and make use of them. Such motivation is non-human, animal-like but also techno-logical (in the sense of *techné*), and its identity in the last instance is radically metaphysical. To understand, control, acquire a sense of home, to surpass the anxiety coming from the *unheimlich* of the real and the outside is to domesticate reality, to produce a tool and give birth to the idea of *techné*, to address the alienation produced by way of sociality and technology: all of this is in its last instance metaphysical.

It is safe to call it philosophical too but without the principle of philosophical sufficiency—thus, non-philosophical. Philosophy is a discipline dedicated to the metaphysical questions adjacent to the sciences, the arts, and the other forms of human practice. However, unlike the other forms of human practice, unlike science for example, it is dedicated not only to resolving metaphysical questions but also to creating a form of universe that will not suffer from any inconsistencies. The world and the real will make perfect sense, they will be reduced to sense, and thus the original radical anxiety of metaphysical nature will be eradicated. The grounding decision on the real and the equation between the real and thought, whereby the former submits to the latter, is the defining characteristic of philosophy, as Laruelle argues (Laruelle, 1989: 231).

Non-philosophy as well as the sciences and the arts permit the presence of metaphysics and its constant challenge by way of subjectivising it rather than "transcending it." By subjectivising, I do not mean individualising but rather appropriating for the species being of humanity. Metaphysics is thus the prime mover of all exploration, at once scientific, artistic, and philosophical. Philosophy is different from the arts and science due to its "decisionism" (on what is real in itself and for us), which dilutes the dyad or rather undermines it by aiming at reducing it to some sense. The real, however, is fundamentally different from sense because it is the object of thought's unilaterally making sense. This is something acknowledged by science and serves as the condition of its grounding posture of thought. Having determined the motivation as metaphysical, let us return to the practice of science, namely the formalisation of language.

Formalism and the possibility of formalising the non-philosophical treatment of metaphysics

By their very nature, metaphysical questions are universal. Universalism is proffered to science by way of its metaphysical kernel. Similarly, metaphysics in its radical form is what provides the universalist basis for non-philosophy or for the project of the scientific practice of philosophy (rid of the principle of sufficiency). Radical metaphysics assumes there is a diversity of cultural or historical forms of subjectivisation (not individualisation), and these forms are thus endowed with their own identity in the last instance. Nonetheless, the metaphysical backdrop conditions the different forms of subjectivisation. Just as science is able to communicate with some form of universal language or aim at greater universality due to the formalism of language and enabled by the metaphysical prime mover, non-philosophy or philosophical science can move beyond the "principle of sufficiency" (Laruelle, 1989: 17).

Thus, universalism is the indispensable condition of science and the scientific practice of philosophy due to the presence of radical metaphysics or metaphysics-without-philosophy. It is also universal thanks to the cognitive procedure of abstraction and the formalisation of language. Different histories, different societies, and political-economic frameworks produce a different culture of scientific practice and different declinations of the formal. This dialectic of the universal and the local, the abstract (in the sense of formal) and the particular, is homologous to the dialectic of synchrony and diachrony in structuralism. Thus, universalism does not dispense with historicity (or "cultural context") but rather presupposes that scientific practice and the formalism of discussion are grounded in history and produce their own specific structures. In order to establish a continuity of conversation, "culturally specific" variations are also subject to formalisation along the trajectory we called, in line with Saussure's model method, "from the concrete to the abstract and back to the concrete." However, instead of the rather vague yet limited concept of "culture," I am suggesting a historical-materialist condition. Universalism is therefore what establishes an inherent link between radical metaphysics and the procedure of formalism.

From formalism to automatism

Formalism can take the form of algorithms, and algorithms are finite automata in a way or are fractions that can stand alone as finite automata. However, logic is also a formalism, but it cannot be reduced to a finite automaton, and it certainly does not comprise a significant element of computer languages qua languages. Basic logical procedures such as syllogisms in computing are reduced to statistical probability rather than the syllogism proper—in spite of emulating the procedure of syllogisms, the conclusion is statistical and is, therefore, not a conclusion or an inference proper (Turing, 1950: 433–460). In computer sciences, the marginal presence of logic and mathematics is a commonplace. Computing is the craft or *techné* of signification, of "cloning the real" into codes or signs, that emulates the physicality of the message and in that way mediates a certain truth or knowledge, but it does not infer, does not resort to logic, and has no interest in metaphysics. It is unable to estimate and compare the environment and its beneficial or harmful effects unless such instruction is generated and is executable based on information input. Plants can think strategically, as a group of researchers from Tübingen University has proven recently (Gruntman et al. 2017). Computers cannot. There is no metaphysical mover, no intentionality, and, ultimately, no material mover such as physicality. There is no *conatus* because the machine is dead. Or, the machine-enabled automaton is highly productive death. In addition, there is neither agency, nor subjectivity, nor subject. Thus, when we speak of machines learning or of their intelligence, we are in fact resorting to metaphors or folk terminology issuing from the manifest image of anthropocentric reality.

As we already pointed out, in computing, the syllogism is present only as the product of the input, which is in fact a statistical result organised in a language that mimics syllogistic reasoning. In the vocabulary of computer science, these sorts of syllogisms are normally referred to as "statistical syllogisms." "If A equals B and if B equals C, then A equals C" can be a syntactic structure in a program language, but it is still a form of processing input data, since the procedure of generalisation or inference is not available to it. Generalisation and particularisation are operations of the formalisation of language that rely on categorical thinking or the ability to create categories and produce them as the result of the practice of thinking. Computing is limited to performing or simulating the available formal operations.

Formalism is in fact a creative and dynamic (rather than predictable and static) process that begins with the concrete or the empirical and with acts of descriptiveness, and then it gradually becomes abstract. In short, formalism is generated by practice, which is ensconced in the empirical, and the evidence of this entrenchment becomes ever less evident as the expression attenuates through ever-greater economisation and abstraction as it clones social relations or the ruling relations ("laws" of a phenomenon), i.e., the structures or other forms of "real abstraction" (Sohn-Rethel, 1978: 13–35). Insofar as it creates itself even when formulae are available and insofar as it is empirically determined, it cannot be reduced to a finite signifying chain or an automaton. However, it is easily translatable into one due to its algorithmic and formulaic constitution.

Formalism is required in order for a language and thought to be scientific. Not every formula or formulaic notion is quantifiable or computable. Nonetheless, the processing of relevant data as well as the construction of syntaxes that clone the algorithmic structure of a science is not only possible but also indispensable for greater productivity.

Categories, natural and technical finite automata, and the non-human self

Categorical thinking and postulates are mediated by means of natural language, or they are in fact a medium or message or an instantiation of language. But are they reducible to it, to the *techné* of language? I would argue that the awkward assemblage we call here the non-human is what initiates and executes these mental products. It is precisely the animal or the physical that is the driving force and thus produces the vector of postulating. Postulation is the work of signification, whereas greater formalisation is always physically supported and empirically confirmed. The formalisation of language determined by matter produces ever-greater abstractions that are not only determined in the last instance by materiality but also return to the material as their object of study. They are neither auto-referential in their interest and in their origin, nor do they seek legitimisation for themselves within themselves (as philosophy does, and some forms of mathematics, logic, and other sciences in their aspects of philosophy). Outsideness or reality as the real (i.e., as not yet syntactically organised) is the object of interest.

The automaton of signification in all its forms, ranging from natural languages to the capitalist value exchange system or the patriarchal exchange of women, from spoken languages to digital languages, is put in motion by forms of animality. When we say animality, we are referring to the prelingual instance of radical subjectivity that poses the questions of naive metaphysics, which is the prime mover of all language and knowledge creation, whether scientific or philosophical. We have explained the concept of radical subjectivity, but let us remember that the latter is a form of selfhood with language at its disposal but is still in the last instance determined by the real of the sheer trauma of being human-in-human, of being determined by or as the real. The mediation of the sheer out-there is what moves art, science, and philosophy, and it takes place at the gates of language—it is prelingual, even though language can be available to it. Therefore, animality and metaphysics are the indispensable element or the fundament of scientific examination and innovation. We have based this claim thus far on Marx, Laruelle, and the structuralists, but we can add to this group some philosophers too, including, and most prominently, Donald Williams and his metaphysics of naturalistic materialism (Williams, 1953). Thus, the agency of artificial intelligence ought to be endowed with these preconditions rather than the ability to "feel" (emotions), which seems to be the fixation of contemporary media and manufacturers.

Let's "attenuate" further the materiality of our observation and arrive at the indispensable minimum of abstraction—let's propose the category that subsumes altogether the animality, humanity, and materiality of the self and is moved by naive metaphysics and desires science. The category that abstracts both living and non-living materiality, conscious life and life without self-reflexivity, nature and technological materiality qua real abstraction, is the category of the physical. Therefore, the "will to knowledge" originates in physicality. But if the motor is some "real abstraction" (such as money), it initiates the motor of physical survival and then, by consequence, language. In this sense, physicality could be further radicalised as an instance of the real, and we can claim that an agency, insofar as it is real or endowed with a conatus, is the motor and the medium of the signifying chain. Yet, the real is modus, not substance, and when seeking to identify the identity in the last instance of the motivation toward the explanation of exteriority and its further formalisation, we are looking at physicality.

As we already explained, the identity in the last instance of the non-human is the radical dyad of the automaton and physicality (both natural and artificial); thus, its identity in the last instance is the dyad in question. The dyad, insofar as it is the radical, minimal, and grounding structure of the (non-human) self, is constituted by two elements that relate unilaterally to one another and are never reconciled in a dialectical unity. "Thought," as Laruelle says, has a unilateral relation toward the real of the outside world it seeks to explain, whereas the real remains indifferent. But thought is not the same as the signifying automaton because it is the product of the "human-in-human" (Laruelle) operating with transcendental material or of the non-human (as we have called it here).

Therefore, in what produces thought, there is a continuity between the two elements of the dyad, which is not the same as unification or unity through unification. The trajectory of continuity is produced by the effects of the determination in the last instance that takes place on the plane of the real or is materially/physically determined. Thus, the physical or the real determines the motivation for signification, and Laruellian "thought" refers to such a mental process that is in the last instance subject to determination by the real. The non-human as the agency of thought seeks to explain the real or the outside world, and the determination that is material vectorially determines the processes of the automaton, yet the two are never "unified." Just as in structuralist linguistics the two elements are unilaterally related whereby the one represents a constitutive other, and just as their unity consists in a non-unity and contradistinction, the same can be said of the non-human dyad.

This is why the participation of the physical in the actions executed by thought (and primarily through and in the form of the signifying automaton) does not imply the "transcendence" of the primitive dyad and its unification into a higher and purely rational entity. Rationalism is the ontologisation of a cognitive faculty and the reification of abstraction. It is in fact the primitive religious procedure of fetishisation. That is why we are not interested in discussions of rationality or rationalism but rather in formalism, which ensures the rigor of investigation and departs from a stance that is essentially scientific, i.e., indifferent toward what kind of ontology may be produced as a result. In fact, it is indifferent to ontology or to an ontologically determined universe.

As already noted, we understand formalism as a movement of thought following the Saussurean trajectory: from the concrete to the abstract and from the abstract back to the concrete. The models we are considering here are provided by the theories of Ferdinand de Saussure, Karl Marx, Luce Irigaray, and François Laruelle. They serve the accurate and exact description and explanation of a reality at hand, with abstraction as one of the necessary cognitive instruments and not as a goal of existence or a parameter of a self-perfecting existence. The goal is to return to the subject matter of study and explain it in its concreteness.

The products of abstraction, the formulaic language solutions, and the artifacts of encoding explain the relations and operations (of "real abstractions") by way of "cloning the real," as Laruelle would say, following "its syntax." Structures, waves, fluxes, and all possible modulations of the real, acts of "realisation" with an inevitably material aspect, even when they are "real abstractions," produce something that Laruelle only tentatively calls a "syntax of the real." It is according to this syntax that thought "clones" the real. It comes down to a very rudimentary description—take, for example, Marx's lengthy and meticulous descriptions of a particular market only to arrive at the general laws of use and surplus value as the result of that very exhaustive description—which is taken to an ever further formalisation of the discussion. As the result of such a process, a formal language suited for the particular syntax is also created. Of course it is the act of cloning of the real that always forecloses—but only in the last instance—to further transcendence, which, in turn, recreates "the syntax of the real" or rather produces a syntax of it and eventually semantics. The *chôra* of the philosophical material serves as the semantic depository for the new syntax and formal language (Laruelle, 1989: 64–69, 133, ff). Such a use of philosophical "conceptual material" implies a non-philosophical treatment of it, one that is defined by a posture of thought, which submits to the real rather than to itself (i.e., to thought) and its self-referential coherence.

Is metaphysical formalism possible, by what means, and what are its limits?

In the *Tractatus Logico-Philosophicus*, Wittgenstein elaborates the procedure of "representation building," which is very similar to what Laruelle calls "cloning of the real": it has to be "linked with reality" (2.1511) and "reach up to it" (2.1511), and, in doing so, it is like a "scale applied to reality," or in German: *Es ist wie ein Maßstab an die Wirklichkeit angelegt* (2.1512). In Laruellian terms, it "clones the real." The "picture" or rather "image" (or in German: *das Bild*) that is "linked to reality" is a fact (Tatsache), as Wittgenstein says (2.141), but only insofar as it is applied to reality as a "scale," only insofar as it "reaches up to reality" (2.1511); and in doing so, it has the "form of representation" or the possibility of a "structure" (2.033).

To apply Wittgenstein's "scale" is to undertake a *descriptiveness* that will lead us to ever more general and ever more abstract notions and ultimately to the creation of categories that enable full formalisation of the discussion. Such a process is sufficiently possible in a universal way for humanity, which enables us to say that universalism is possible without or beyond cultural hegemony. The sign is a code that "clones the real" or generates the identity in the last instance of the object of study, and that is why it is transcendentally minimal and fundamentally descriptive (Laruelle, 2014: 179). Identity in the last instance is normally a concept. This concept is in the last instance determined by the real or a particular real. In the study of non-philosophy or the non-philosophical study of philosophical material, we are interested in the identity in the last instance, but due to the fact that it is a clone is why we are also interested in the real out of which it was cloned.

The radical metaphysical concept, one that is not the product of the discipline of thought called philosophy but a direct clone of an experience of exteriority, the horror and wonder of being-in-the-out-there, being-before-the-other, the horror and wonder facing the difference between living and non-living entities, the horror of the indifference of the non-living other and of the out-there, the horror and wonder before nature as the out-there that is both living and non-living, acting as a living non-entity or the real alive: all of these ideas are direct clones of the experience of the real or of the real insofar as this experience is a non-reflected real. And they all resort to language, but they can dispense with it, too. They precede every utterance yet urge all utterances. They therefore initiate and require signification. The more formal the signification, the more narratively minimal and the more precise the cloning of the experience of the real in the form of metaphysical wonderful horror. The path begins with the concrete, ascends to the highest possible abstraction—and, to arrive there, narration is indispensable— only to reach the most minimal expression that signifies (i.e., mediates) with the highest possible exactness the pure form of the real or the clone.

Let us consider the following model of binary signification proposed by Wittgenstein that condenses some of the most basic laws of logic and operations of thought constitutive of philosophy:

> The truth-functions of every number of elementary propositions can be written in a schema of the following kind: $\sim \supset \subset \wedge \vee$
>
> (TTTT) (p, q) Tautology (if p then p, and if q then q) $[p \supset p . q \supset q]$
>
> (FTTT) (p, q) in words: Not both p and q. $[\sim (p . q)]$
>
> (TFTT) (p, q) „ „ If q then p. $[q \supset p]$
>
> (TTFT) (p, q) „ „ If p then q. $[p \supset q]$
>
> (TTTF) (p, q) „ „ p or q. $[p \vee q]$
>
> (FFTT) (p, q) „ „ Not q. $[\sim q]$
>
> (FTFT) (p, q) „ „ Not p. $[\sim p]$
>
> (FTTF) (p, q) „ „ p or q, but not both. $[p . \sim q : \vee : q . \sim p]$
>
> (TFFT) (p, q) „ „ If p, then q; and if q, then p. $[p \equiv q]$
>
> (TFTF) (p, q) „ „ p
>
> (TTFF) (p, q) „ „ q
>
> (FFFT) (p, q) „ „ Neither p nor q. $[\sim p . \sim q \text{ or } p | q]$

(FFTF) (p, q) „ „ p and not q. [p. ~q]
(FTFF) (p, q) „ „ q and not p. [q. ~p]
(TFFF) (p, q) „ „ p and q. [p. q]
(FFFF) (p, q) Contradiction (p and not p; and q and not q.) [p. ~p, q. ~q]
(Wittgenstein, *Tractatus Logico-Philosophicus*: 5.101)

The entire set of logical operations is reducible to the order of two signs: "T" and "F" (insofar as F equals –T). The possible combinations of the two signs in an endless chain do not even involve any algorithm or syllogism; there is no procedure of inference—there is no logic, only statistically possible correct and incorrect or true and false statements. They are either true or false depending on how they (unilaterally) relate to the real, depending on whether they constitute a scale (*Maßstab*) or not. What is at stake here is the mere marking of the reality of p and q and their relations by way of "cloning" it into a series of true and false signs. The signs should recreate an image ("*Bild*") of the reality that is its scale (*Maßstab*) or clone. The signs themselves in their material sequentiality do not represent anything except cloning the physical sequentiality of the real taking place, through simple "yes" and "no" or "true" and "false" (or rather negation of true), whereby the physical reproduction of the real via the workings of the transcendental (i.e., through language) enables the second transcendental—the representation or image (*Bild*) of the structure of the real. The latter is what scientific invention (as well as the commonsensical and any other form of intelligence) requires. Wittgenstein writes:

This connexion of the elements of the picture is called its structure, and the possibility of this structure is called the form of representation of the picture. (2.150)[1]

---

[1] Put in context and in the German original: 2.150 Dass sich die Elemente des Bildes in bestimmter Art und Weise zu einander verhalten stellt vor, dass sich die Sachen so zueinander verhalten. Dieser Zusammenhang der Elemente des Bildes heisse seine Struktur und ihre Möglichkeit seine Form der Abbildung.

Further in the text he explains:

> The gramophone record, the musical thought, the score, the waves of sound, all stand to one another in that pictorial internal relation, which holds between language and the world. To all of them the logical structure is common. (4014)

That pictorial relation, although preceding language and being external to the world, nonetheless possesses a "logical structure." The structure possesses a certain logic because it is the *Maßstab* or the clone of the real, but its very possibility is provided by the material practice of signification on the material appearance of the real, by the practice of signalisation of true and false in which, on the other hand, there is no logic:

> It is clear that to the complex of the signs "F" and "T" no object (or complex of objects) corresponds; any more than to horizontal and vertical lines or to brackets. There are no "logical objects." (4.441)[2]

There are "truth possibilities," and he proposes their combinations instead of logic in this binary language (Wittgenstein: 4.442). *The signaling of true and false, present and absent, is no different from any other practice of language it seems.* If language mediates not only the real as it appears but the reality of the true and the false, then it constitutes a second language of a doubling or mirroring kind that frames the reality of the cloning of the real (in other words, a cloning to the second power). Such could be the model of the full formalisation of a non-philosophical language applied to the real world in view of explaining its workings or that of radical metaphysics. By way of the radicalisation of the concept and arriving at its identity in the last instance

---

[2] 4.441 Es ist klar, dass dem Komplex der Zeichen „F" und „W" kein Gegenstand (oder Komplex von Gegenständen) entspricht; so wenig, wie den horizontalen und vertikalen Strichen oder den Klammern.—„Logische Gegenstände" gibt es nicht.

and the real as determination in the last instance, what can be established is a language that signifies the presence or absence of cloning the real in a philosophical or metaphysical account. However, it seems that such a procedure could constitute something more akin to an algorithm serving a function in the language of radical metaphysics rather than a foundation for a language *sui generis*. In this sense, I concur with Anne-Françoise Schmid when she argues that "the integrated objects" of non-philosophically mediated interdisciplinary science are not "the realization of possibilities, but that they first and foremost propose impossibility, for which one has to generate new relations between knowledge. A little like in algebras of extension, where the impossible solution of an equation gives us the rules to construct a new set allowing for the interpretation of the solution in a new way" (Schmid, 2015: 66).

Let's take the question of gender, namely its relation to sexual difference, biology, and sexuality. Is its identity in the last instance determined by the opposition to the concept of sex or by its differentiation from it? Is its determination in the last instance relational? Gender is determined by the material reality of performativity. The performance in question concerns social roles determined by their function of sexuality. The concept of performativity thus describes or clones the reality of such a social function. Reproduction is irrelevant for the identity in the last instance of the concept and the reality it clones. Gender as a role or modality of performativity is in the last instance determined by the reality of socially assigned sexual roles or subject formations. In the same way that society is not a stable and static category but a historical one, gender does move and transform, and there is no certainty of its sense and of its essence. Thus, in the last instance, the determining real of performativity is a stable category, whereas gender formations or subject positions are mutable ones. Socially assigned sexual roles or subject positions oscillate between two relatively stable poles of semantic contents, i.e., masculinity and femininity. Unstable and mutable gender configurations produce a multiplicity out of the given binary. In this sense, performativity produces a multiplicity of structures stemming from and branching out of the binary of femininity and masculinity. Femininity and masculinity as opposing poles and elements of the constitutive binary are transcendental: they are the concepts and semantics derived from the two reproductively determined types of the species being of humanity. The following diagram (Figure 1) is a summary of the discussion at hand produced by Etienne Brouzes, presented here with his permission:

Gender [Concept] is determined by its identity in the last instance, which is [<] performativity [concept/clone]; performativity is determined by [<] the real of the social distribution of sexualised subject positions [real/real abstraction]; the distribution of sexual subject positions (or "gendered roles") is determined by [<] the binary structural organisation of femininity and masculinity [real/real abstraction], which, in turn, is determined by [<] the reproductive reality of a human society [the real as the physical determination in the last instance]. The procedure of "philosophical impoverishment" (Laruelle) is that of an ever-greater abstraction to arrive at the "concrete" (or in Laruelle's case, the "real"), and it thus follows the second leg of Saussure's trajectory. It enables us to

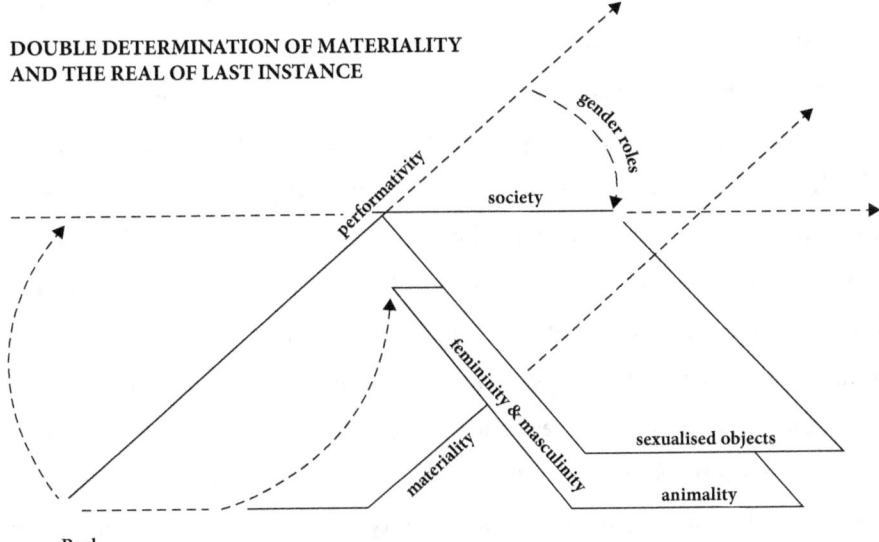

FIGURE 1 *Double determination of materiality and the real of last instance.*

non-philosophically recreate the transcendental minimum of a concept and, beginning with the identity in the last instance while immanently correlating with the determining real, to create a realist account.

Such is the non-philosophical proposal. The Marxian addition to it would be to radicalise the real by arriving at its physical or material cause. One ought to engage in a metaphysical choice in order to decide whether materiality will be the determining last instance, whether it will be the real that directly affects the clone, which could be a real abstraction (such as an aspect of social relations). It is also an ideological choice, not necessarily epistemically indispensable for the realist method but consistent with it. Beginning with the concrete of the basic structure of performativity or the determining binary that branches out into more complicated structures, we can determine the clone of gender: it refers to the possible complexities of the structural branches of subject positions and the declination from the ideal "feminine" and "masculine."

As Saussure said, the ideal phoneme does not exist in reality, but it is indispensable to explain the real phonemes as declinations from the ideal; so, by homology, the gendered positions and the declinations from the ideal are what we encounter in the concreteness of the social organisation of sexuality. If the species being of humanity dispenses with these roles and projects some post-gender form of social organisation of sexuality and, by consequence, of sexual reproduction, the concept and reality of gender will probably become obsolete. If a reversal of economic logic in patriarchy is possible, these roles will become obsolete along with bourgeois marriage itself, including the parenting that goes hand in hand with it. Gender roles are the effects of the bourgeois structure of society and its organisation of social reproduction. While in the given political-economic order, the marginal formations of gender constitute realities (and the real qua real abstractions) that suffer oppression or exploitation based on their identity in the last instance but determined by the materiality of their material vulnerability. The centrality of the theme of "gender as identity" in left-wing political discourse nowadays serves rather than undermines the given political-economic order. Conversely, to focus on exploitation, commodification, and reduction to resources for surplus value (or simply value) is to focus on the material reality of the marginal subject positions determined by gender. Such novel repositioning of the gender-related social and political-economic battles could provide a basis for some tangible change in the *status quo*.

Possibilities and limits of non-philosophical formalism

In the *Introduction to Non-Marxism* ([2000] 2016), Laruelle expressly states that the formalism of a "different sort," one following the model of quantum theory departing from the procedure of subtraction rather than logical formalism, is possible for non-Marxism (180). In this chapter, however, we are interested not only in what formalism can provide for non-Marxism and non-philosophy but instead also the opposite—what non-philosophy (of both Laruelle and Marx) can offer for the expansion of the possibilities of formalism.

Let us attempt to formalise the procedure of "philosophical impoverishment" according to Laruelle that will enable us to arrive at the "transcendental minimum" whose semantic contents can be communicated across the sciences. In fact, such impoverishment will enable what Laruelle calls the scientific approach to philosophy as material of study. Although such procedure has not been elaborated by Marx, his project of establishing a "science" on matters that are usually dealt with philosophically has been executed through an exemplary formalisation of empirical observation, one initially operating with philosophical concepts only to impoverish the latter and arrive at the science of political economy. This kind of science shall, as Marx argues, lead us to the full "realisation of the species being of humanity" or communism, and such a goal is essentially metaphysical.

> Communism as the positive transcendence of private property as human self-estrangement, and therefore as the real appropriation of the human essence by and for man; communism therefore as the complete return of man to himself as a social (i.e., human) being—a return accomplished consciously and embracing the entire wealth of previous development [...] Communism is the riddle of history solved, and it knows itself to be this solution. (Marx, 1959: "Private Property and Communism")

The formula that will enable this is M-C-M with its subsequent "arborescence" into formulae concerning surplus value and the socialist response to it, which is elaborated in the third volume of *Capital*. In addition to the models proffered by Marx's political economy and Laruelle's non-philosophy, we can draw on structuralism as the science of accomplished formalism concerning the signification or signs and the "technology of making" sense. The proposed steps in the procedure of impoverishment as conceived by Laruelle can be enriched or supplemented by Marx's materialism (or "physicalist realism") without causing any distortion in the initial idea. Also, the concept of the "clone" can be explained through the structuralist notion of sign and the automaton of the signifying chain, which will enable us to circumvent the redundancy of anthropocentric argumentation.

Let us assume there is a string of steps, which establish an adequate formula that ensures stability and the results that can be empirically corroborated. Also, let us examine if such a formula allows the development of an "algorithm"—or whether it is endowed with inherent possibilities to produce predictable and possibly automatable results—that will render radical metaphysics predictable, readable, and communicable to other sciences. Outside the philosophical universe and inside the realm of *techné*, automaticity is not a goal in itself and is not sufficient for scientific exploration but rather ensures exactitude and corroboration from the real as the determining exteriority. It also ensures the increased productivity of scientific investigation and is one of its unavoidable parts but not its "essence" to which the entire realm of science would be reduced.

One of the themes we seek to apply such an approach with the goal of arriving at the radical immanence that motivates some of the major technological projects is the insidious presence of spontaneous anthropocentrism. An automaton that perpetuates its operation without human intervention, a recreation of human subjectivity without the natural human, a recreation of life itself without life, an existence without vitality or vitalism, the transcendence of the natural as the "inferior form of existence" only to recreate it rationally—all of this sounds like nothing but metaphysics. It not only sounds so, but it is so by definition: it will lead us to desubjectivised Reason as the prime mover of all existence. And, according to such philosophical dreams, this Reason ought to be absolute, and the rationality or scientific reason of a mortal inventor also ought to be surpassed. For what purpose? The purpose obviously transcends the interests of a practical scientific nature. (I am referring to the practice of science and its immanent rules but also to the social function of science consisting in improving the conditions of the species being of humanity.) Again, such a purpose or goal is metaphysical.

If we are to treat it non-philosophically or scientifically, the metaphysical core of some philosophical-scientific projects ought to be radicalised, stripped of philosophy as a self-encircling system, and the posture of thought ought to step outside the realm defined by philosophical sufficiency. The bare and naive clone of metaphysical experience ought to be treated non-philosophically, which will enable us to arrive at its determination in the last instance. By doing so, we should be able to attempt a reconceptualisation of the syntax of the clones in correlation with the real (of that experience), rather than resorting to the self-referential laws of a philosophical doctrine. The new set of radical concepts cloned from the real of metaphysical experience will be tested against practice, and the measurement of practice will be formalised. Formalisation does not necessarily imply automation. Laruelle seems to rely on a similar assumption when he writes:

> Even qua automatism, the One is perceptible only through these effects of discourse or its practice, not in itself, since it's not a thing or intellectual intuition. Michel Henry couldn't keep himself from giving it an identifiable content in transcendence. But this isn't algorithmic automatism, which is integrally visible and given in a finitary and quasi-geometrical way. Scientific automatism is that of transcendence, but it's not philosophical; it thus supposes a metalanguage and is undoubtedly the complex form of the scientific relation to the real. (Laruelle, 2013b)

A formulaic syntax or formalisation of the language of radical metaphysics, or of the science that clones the real of metaphysical experience, would ensure a relatively universal and relatively stable character of certain procedures that yield results communicable to other sciences. "Identity in the last instance—Clone—Real (Real abstraction/> Real physical): Transcendental" is a simple string of conceptual radicalisation following Laruelle's prescripts (supplemented by Marxian "physicality" or "materiality"), thus enabling us to arrive at the determination in the last instance of a *philosopheme*. This string is a rudimentary formulaic expression that seeks to communicate identity in the last instance determined by the real (which, in turn, is determined by the physical) in order to measure the level of philosophical declination from a non-philosophical cloning. Whether or not a proper "algorithmisation" of this kind is possible (or needed) remains to be seen and demonstrated.

There is, however, content that escapes formalism (and most certainly computability): in the last instance, the real escapes full signification. Radical metaphysics (let's reiterate) deals with the real of experience, and in that experience the real plays an active role while language is germinal, in an initial stage of alienation from the real. One can only clone the effects that betray a certain syntax, but the rest remains enmeshed with the real, and poetic and philosophical language becomes unavoidable. This remainder is incomputable and probably escapes formulaic expression, too. Thus, not only philosophy, but also non-philosophy, Marxian science, and structrualism as well need to allow the limitations of formalisation by affirming the mentioned fact and the reservoir of narration it enables.

> Subjectivity, whose phenomenal appearing in-One is the fabric of the subject effect, is included in this philosophy-form in particular. This fully excludes that the determined effects, which are of philosophical extraction, can be produced by an automatic system, at least provided that philosophy's transcendental mechanism can itself escape from this automatism and this reduction to a simple mechanism. It's transcendence in general that excludes philosophy's reduction to an algorithm. Now, one can obviously pose the problem of the possible degree of automation of transcendence, which is philosophy's transcendental nerve. But to the extent that it continues on (albeit transformed) in the subject, philosophy limits the chances of automaticity and formalism. (Laruelle, 2013b)

The fantasy of covering the entire realm of reality with knowledge and that "true" knowledge would be the full penetration of the real, grasping and submitting the latter to its authority to the extent that the real becomes nothing but an image of knowledge and is fully transposed onto the plane of transcendence, and is, as we know, a philosophical tendency. The notion of the "principle of sufficient philosophy" (or PSP) proposed by Laruelle refers precisely to such a category of ambition in the endeavors of explaining reality that surrounds us and constitutes us, too.

It remains unclear to what extent the formalisation of the scientific language of philosophy is possible and to what degree its automation would be necessary. Philosophical systems do function as automata that produce predictable results according to a certain "statistical logic." What we are seeking, however, is the formalisation of categories that transcend the unchecked anthropomorphic spontaneity of classical oppositions (e.g., nature and technology, body and mind). We propose the distinction—although not necessarily the opposition—

of the physical and the automaton (and both can be categories of either "natural" viz. organic origin or synthetically produced viz. technologically enabled) as sufficiently formal to enable a productive dialogue with other sciences and contribute effectively to the political discussions of post-humanism. Those categories are universal yet can and should be applied locally and in specific areas of study. The procedures of this type of universalism can be far more politically productive in explaining cultural specificities and also in giving voice to particularities, thereby avoiding any hegemony.

We find a model of such a concept and method in Sylvia Wynter's analysis of "classarchy," which is not merely a metaphor but rather a formal category that can be used for cross-cultural analysis, thereby enabling a form of universalism that is profoundly sensitive to cultural specificities. This is a category that cuts across "culturalities" along a certain vector of universality. In fact, it serves as an explanatory instrument that gives an account of "cultural" differences as a relation to the universal category of classarchy. Classarchy is a middle-class model of humanity that can have either its liberal humanist definition or its Marxist-Leninist one: either way, man-as-father "provides the organising principle" of a cultural order and acts as the general equivalent of identity. Social roles and their localisms are variations of the same principle. All variations of this model are underpinned by capital as the "General Equivalent Signifier of Identity and Status." The fact that its origin lies in Western metaphysics does not make it less universal, because capital or "non-landed property" as "the Place of the Phallus-the-Symbolic-Penis" or "the General Equivalent of Capital Man-as-Father" guarantees its universal applicability (under the condition of a globalised world) (Wynter, 1982: 3).

The categories of the automaton as something that is not reducible to machines and that cuts across worlds human and non-human, animal and machinic, along with that of physicality as the determination in the last instance of the real and of its transcendental rendition (the material), are subjected to non-philosophical radicalisation in order to arrive at their pure form, which is transferable and applicable to different objects of analysis, one that can find its formulaic expression. Non-philosophical radicalisation consists in the above-presented procedure of arriving at a transcendental minimum representing determination in the last instance. Radical concepts are identity in the last instance, which is a certain transcendental that has been "cloned" from the real (Laruelle, 2014: 51). A concept is never immanence, but it can be "affected by immanence" (Laruelle). We call these kinds of concepts "radical concepts." Furthermore, these concepts can be subjected to formalisation and assume formulaic expression.

3

Subjectivity as inherently philosophical entity and the third person's perspective

In Marx's philosophical writings, in particular *German Ideology* and *Philosophical Economic Manuscripts 1844*, but also in his political economy we witness a project of transcending philosophy by means of its own conceptual material. In other words, he seeks to reverse the very relationship between the real and philosophy by postulating a theory, which grounds itself and any other theory or scientific investigation in the material, the real, in praxis and in direct, "physical and sensuous" experience. The latter strings of topics are recurrent philosophical themes that cut across the entire opus of Karl Marx and are not limited to a period. In other words, they are not divided by an epistemological break. I concur with Michel Henry when he argues that there is a constant interest in philosophy as well as a consistent treatment of it throughout Marx's opus (Henry, 1983). Marx's "philosophical project," is, arguably, a project of post-philosophy. Henry's argument is similar except he chooses to call Marx's humanism philosophy dealing with questions of "subjectivity and individualism" (Henry, 1983: 12). I will argue here that Marx deals with the question of subjectivity only to point out to it as the symptom of what is fundamentally flawed in philosophy in general. The apex of the fallacy or the point of climax of what Marx seems to identify as pathological in all hitherto philosophy is found in Hegel. Marx never revised his stance on Hegel and the reconciliation between the two thinkers has been carried out by Lenin. I propose that we concentrate in this chapter on the question of "subjectivity" in the way it is addressed in Marx's own opus, namely in his *Critique of Hegel's Philosophy in General* (Marx, 1959) as well as in *The German Ideology* (1968), and explore how the main issues raised there resurface in the later works. We will concentrate more closely on the "problem of philosophy in general" he sought to tackle by his "march toward reality, toward the 'real material presuppositions' which constitute the teleology and the content of his philosophical reflection" (Henry, 1983: 13).

Nature, the capitalist automaton, and subjectivism of philosophy

I concur with Henry when he argues that there is no such thing as "epistemological break" in Marx as the above-presented themes are recurrent and underpin the entire opus organising it as a coherent whole. Marx's humanism has always been about materialism, which, in turn, Marx often and unequivocally reduces to naturalism. The latter is true not only of the early writings such as *Philosophical Economic Manuscripts of 1844* (*PEM 1844*) but also of *German Ideology* and *Grundrisse*. Marx's treatment of the concept of use value (1973: 114) is grounded in the attempt of materialist or physicalist vindication of value as such—in order for a value not to be a self-standing abstraction, it draws its sense from the physical use of the produce, food, shelter, etc. Each commodity is produced to serve the "physical and sensuous" (*PEM 1844*) needs. Such use of produce is called "use value" and it is determined by concrete "bodily form" (Marx, *Capital II*, Vol. 2, Chapter 22). Use value is nurturing and protecting the physical self (as "selfhood" itself is in the last instance determined by physicality), and that is why Marx exclaims in *PEM 1844*: "This communism, as fully developed naturalism, equals humanism, and as fully developed humanism equals naturalism." The same argument resurfaces in the first volume of *Capital* and its critique of commodity fetishism, or critique of "abstracted materiality" or the abstraction of materiality, and, finally, in Marx's critique of automation of abstracted human labor in *Grundrisse* (1973: 618–630).

> But, once adopted into the production process of capital, the means of labour passes through different metamorphoses, whose culmination is the machine, or rather, an automatic system of machinery (system of machinery: the automatic one is merely its most complete, most adequate form, and alone transforms machinery into a system), set in motion by an automaton, a moving power that moves itself; this automaton consisting of numerous mechanical and intellectual organs, so that the workers themselves are cast merely as its conscious linkages. In the machine, and even more in machinery as an automatic system, the use value, i.e. the material quality of the means of labour, is transformed into an existence adequate to fixed capital and to capital as such; and the form in which it was adopted into the production process of capital, the direct means of labour, is superseded by a form posited by capital itself and corresponding to it. In no way does the machine appear as the individual worker's means of labour. Its distinguishing characteristic is not in the least, as with the means of labour, to transmit the worker's activity to the object; this activity, rather, is posited in such a way that it merely transmits the machine's work, the machine's action, on to the raw material—supervises it and guards against interruptions. (Marx, 1973: 620–621)

According to Marx, the industrial production, in its materiality, which includes the human body and mind too, is part of the universal machine of capital and it is a self-sustained universe without the need of human skill to guide it. In a way, it emulates the "*abstract egoist—egoism* raised in its pure abstraction" of philosophy (1959: *Critique of Hegel's Philosophy in General*), i.e., the subjectivity centered reason as philosophical humanism. The prime mover of the capitalist automaton (of "value production") is generalised Reason shaped by philosophical humanism and the "post-" in the prefix does not move it beyond its determination in the last instance. This self-standing abstraction is the core of capitalist ontology based on the simple gesture of generalisation of a purely philosophical abstraction of *human subjectivity*, epitomised in Hegel's Absolute Spirit (Marx, 1959; 1968). Humans are the necessary conscious elements built into the automaton so they can serve the function of the conscious linkages of oversight of the automated operations. The worker is part of the process only to be used as a form of means of production, as part of the "fixed capital" or the material required for the machine (of capital) to endlessly circulate (Marx, 1973: 621). But the cycle itself that is perpetuated endlessly is a "senseless abstraction" that purports to be self-standing.

> The circle Money—Commodity—Commodity—Money, which we drew from the analysis of circulation, would then appear to be merely an arbitrary and senseless abstraction, roughly as if one wanted to describe the life cycle as Death—Life—Death; although even in the latter case it could not be denied that the constant decomposition of what has been individualised back into the elemental is just as much a moment of the process of nature as the constant individualisation of the elemental. (Marx, 1973: 138)

And, yet again, writes Marx, the "senseless abstraction" of Death-Life-Death has at least some relation to nature referring to the process of "decomposition" of the individual (body and self) back to the "elemental." The reference to a natural process reduces the "senselessness" of the Death-Life-Death abstraction. "Money-Commodity-Money" is, however, irreparably senseless as it does not find its determination in the last instance in the material as natural. If a value is merely surplus value rather than use value, viz. value that is materially realised, it forms a circuit of an auto-referential abstraction: use value is not what moves capital but rather the surplus value or, simply, pure value. That is why the exchange comes down to M-M', which is the reason for Marx to identify it as "senseless"—the tautology is evident.

Moreover, it is senseless because abstraction cannot pretend to be other than an intellectual means, a faculty and instrument of cognition, a process that is materially determined in its last instance. (This argument is not made in line with any school of philosophical thought but is rather based on scientific data concerning the "material" mind and feelings are made of nerves, DNA, and the rest of the notorious "physical banality." Although it does correspond with Marx's claim that "spirit" is conditioned by "nerves and muscles" and thus the "depressed spirit" of wage laborer is explained throughout his oeuvre.) It is neither a purpose nor a cause—reality is material and, to Marx, that also means natural. Thus "spirit," "reason," or "meaning" is not only materially enabled but it is also its effect. Marx makes sure that his critique of the flawed metaphysics of capitalism is not misread as romantic vitalism: the contempt, and therefore the epistemic fallacy to disregard "the bodily aspects" of human production, including the means of production, is what underpins capitalist logic as moved by surplus value only (whereas the use value remains outside the capitalist equation). All of this "bodily reality" ought to be transformed into the self-standing abstraction called "capital" and the creation of surplus value, as explained in the quote below:

> In the process of production the purchased labour-power now forms a part of the functioning capital, and the labourer himself serves here merely as a special bodily form of this capital, distinguished from its elements existing in the bodily form of means of production. During the process, by expending his labour-power, the labourer adds value to the means of production which he converts into products equal to the value of his

> labour-power (exclusive of surplus-value); he therefore reproduces for the capitalist in the form of commodities that portion of his capital which has been, or has to be, advanced by him for wages, produces for him an equivalent of the latter; hence he reproduces for the capitalist that capital which the latter can "advance" once more for the purchase of labour-power. (Marx, *Capital II:* Chapter 19)

The subjection of the worker, of her body and "spirit" made of "muscle and nerves" (Marx, 1959), to the automated machine of capital is subjection of nature to the senselessness of the M-C-M abstraction. This concern as central stretches throughout Marx's opus, beginning with his early writings, surfacing in the *Communist Manifesto* of 1848 (Marx and Engels, 1969b) and, as demonstrated, reappearing in the *Grundrisse* of 1857–8. The contradiction of the capitalist-bourgeois conception and practice of production becomes evident precisely through the tension between capital both as automation and as the physical reality of machines used in the production, on the one hand, and the worker as physical reality and nature, on the other hand. This question, whose nature is apparently metaphysical, is tackled in what is supposed to be a political-economic program of *The Communist Manifesto*. The metaphysics of the tension between body and idea is transformed into socioeconomic and political programmatic stance:

> Owing to the extensive use of machinery, and to the division of labour, the work of the proletarians has lost all individual character, and, consequently, all charm for the workman. He becomes an appendage of the machine, and it is only the most simple, most monotonous, and most easily acquired knack, that is required of him. (Marx and Engels, 1969b: 18)

The consequences are of the category of internal contradictions of capitalism that can amount to a condition for a socialist reversal as the tension described below cannot be sustained in perpetuity:

In proportion, therefore, as the repulsiveness of the work increases, the wage decreases. Nay more, in proportion as the use of machinery and division of labour increases, in the same proportion the burden of toil also increases, whether by prolongation of the working hours, by the increase of the work exacted in a given time or by increased speed of machinery, etc. (Marx and Engels, 1969b: 18)

The contradiction can be solved by seizing the means of production in order to reverse the very metaphysics of capitalism: endlessly increased productivity and endlessly exploited nature will make no sense because use value—or simply the practice of use with no reference to "value"—will replace surplus value as the prime mover of production. Use value is determined by materiality and exhausted in its material consumption or consumability. Such should be the metaphysical reversal to be brought about by communism conceived as "the riddle of history solved" (Marx, 1959). Indeed, what the mature Marx presents as the solution to capitalism is about the "humanism as naturalism" thesis of the early works and, in his own words, "Communism is the riddle of history solved, and it knows itself to be this solution" (Marx, 1959). And indeed, concurring with Michel Henry, let us reiterate, there was never such thing as an "epistemological break" and, therefore, the triad of humanism-naturalism-communism reappears as a minimal structure of his political project in the later works too (as demonstrated above).

An interpretation such as this [referring to the "break"] is not only abusive, it is categorically denied by Marx himself, when in 1859, with the distance of intervening years, he makes the irrevocable judgment in the preface to the *Critique of Political Economy* by which the radical critique of German thought as well as the clear awareness of its results are attributed to *The German Ideology* [...] "When in the spring of 1845, he [Engels] too came to live in Brussels, we decided to set forth together our conception as opposed to the ideological one of German philosophy, in fact to settle accounts with our former philosophical conscience. The intention was carried out in the form of a critique of post-Hegelian philosophy. The manuscript, two large octavo volumes, had long ago reached the publishers in Westphalia when we were informed that owing to changed circumstances it could not be printed. We abandoned the manuscript to the gnawing criticism of the mice all the more willingly since we had achieved our main purpose—self-clarification." (Henry, 1983: 10)

Henry cites the preface to a much later work by Marx in reference to a work of the already mature phase, i.e., *The German Ideology*, to demonstrate that Marx himself declares continuity between his early philosophical writings and the themes and methods pursued in his later works. *The German Ideology*, even if not published during Marx's lifetime (due to a publisher's failure to do so), has served its main purpose—philosophical "self-clarification," states Marx himself. The self-clarification, apparently, amounts to (a) the development of a method that enables an exit from philosophy's circular self-enclosure, (b) a grounding of a post-philosophical science of the species being of humanity, and (c) a method that is radically materialist and, as a consequence, also naturalist. In doing away with Hegel, Marx is doing away with philosophy and he says so himself explicitly and unequivocally in *The German Ideology*.

> German criticism has, right up to its latest efforts, never quitted the realm of philosophy. Far from examining its general philosophic premises, the whole body of its inquiries has actually sprung from the soil of a definite philosophical system, that of Hegel. Not only in their answers but in their very questions there was a mystification. (Marx, 1968)

The shift toward science Marx proposes is a shift toward a science issuing from philosophy and, therefore, drawing on its conceptual material. It is a science of humanity grounding itself in humanity's auto-referential narrative par excellence—philosophy. It seems there is, as if were, a perfect homology in structure and substance with Laruelle's non-philosophy: philosophy ought to turn into science that deals with the human universe whereby philosophy and world are synonymous. Therefore, both philosophy and the world are not examined in their totality but rather treated as "chôra" or cosmologically unorganised material to be studied in its unilaterality. Indeed, there is no surprise in this realisation as Laruelle himself reveals in his *Introduction to Non-Marxism* to be heavily indebted to Marx in the development of his method of non-philosophy and, therefore, also its later variation: non-standard philosophy (2014: 11, 14, 73, 174). Just as Laruelle proposes a science of humanity as the result of his non-philosophical radicalisation of philosophy so does Marx speak of humanism grounded in praxis and, consequentially, nature.

In order to arrive at a scientific account of humanity one needs to posit it axiomatically in a way that is fundamentally different if not opposite from the one that defines philosophy: the real and the real of humanity are in the last instance determined by matter or physicality and praxis, and, in giving an account of them, the thinking subject submits to the real rather than to any philosophy. Such is the position of Laruelle's non-philosophy but also of Marx: "The production of ideas, of conceptions, of consciousness, is at first directly interwoven with the material activity and the material intercourse of men, the language of real life. Conceiving, thinking, the mental intercourse of men, appear at this stage as the direct efflux of their material behaviour" (Marx, 1968: 6). The axiom at issue proffers a sufficient postulation of a post-philosophical project of formulating a method of human sciences. In order for such a project to succeed, as previously discussed, Marx insists a "third party's" perspective of theorising ought to be adopted.

"Subjectivity" and its status in philosophy and capitalism

Marx's claim is that the fundamental problem of philosophy is precisely its subjectivism and, therefore, production of a thought that is one of "the universal egoist," or rather the human self that has abstracted itself from the physical world in the form of "self-consciousness" cannot study either itself or the world objectively, due to its inability to posit itself as objective reality vis-à-vis other realities, third parties so to speak. Philosophical reason, culminating in Hegel's philosophy, as Marx insists, posits the objective world subjectively; i.e., it submits the exterior reality to the constitution of the subject as self-consciousness, which, in turn, posits itself as a self-standing entity substituting objectivity. Self-consciousness treats the exterior reality or the objective world as mere material of its constitution. Also, the self-standing reality or even entity of self-consciousness is to be understood as a superior form of objectivity. It is the objectivity more objective than objectivity itself, just as in Laruelle's critique philosophy appears to produce a superior form of the real—the being (an amphibology of the real and truth or truth as the real), one more real than the real itself. We are not speaking here of Marx being blind to the problem of *noumenon* or Laruelle's inability to recognise the foreclosure of the real, but quite the contrary: the foreclosure is admitted and what the thinking subject can do is submit itself to its structure and syntax and attempt to "code" it, mediate it, transpose it onto the plane of the transcendental or language, recreate it as sign. Such transpositions are the material praxis enabling the transcendental product of describing and explaining exterior reality or the real. The description will be scientific—and I would add artistic too—if the subject is capable of conceiving itself as an objective reality, not the other way around (adopt the third party's perspective). Such is the basis of Marx's non-anthropocentric scientific method and, yet again, one determined by humanity as its identity in the last instance, as elaborated in the chapter "Opposition of the Materialist and Idealist Outlook" in *German Ideology*.

> This method of approach is not devoid of premises. It starts out from the real premises and does not abandon them for a moment. Its premises are men, not in any fantastic isolation and rigidity, but in their actual, empirically perceptible process of development under definite conditions. As soon as this active life-process is described, history ceases to be a collection of dead facts as it is with the empiricists (themselves still abstract), or an imagined activity of imagined subjects, as with the idealists. Where speculation ends—in real life—there real, positive science begins: the representation of the practical activity, of the practical process of development of men. (Marx, 1968)

Seeking to establish knowledge of the exterior reality in a way that mirrors the subject, both the individual and the assumed universal (human) subject, is, as already discussed, a philosophical gesture par excellence. If, conversely, one adopts Marx's method, one should also seek to conceive of themselves as being an object to a third person's gaze amidst an objective world.

> Whenever real, corporeal man, man with his feet firmly on the solid ground, man exhaling and inhaling all the forces of nature, posits his real, objective essential powers as alien objects by his externalisation, it is not the act of positing which is the subject in this process: it is the subjectivity of objective essential powers, whose action, therefore, must also be something objective. An objective being acts objectively, and he would not act objectively if the objective did not reside in the very nature of his being. He only creates or posits objects, because he is posited by objects—because at bottom he is nature. In the act of positing, therefore, this objective being does not fall from his state of "pure activity" into a creating of the object; on the contrary, his objective product only confirms his objective activity, his activity as the

activity of an objective, natural being. (Marx, 1959: "Critique of Hegel's Philosophy in General")[1]

Or put differently:

To be objective, natural and sensuous, and at the same time to have object, nature and sense outside oneself, or oneself to be object, nature and sense for a third party, is one and the same thing. (Marx, 1959: "Critique of Hegel's Philosophy in General")

To posit the contrary is to pursue philosophy, argues Marx in *The German Ideology* (Marx, 1968). The thought that is centered on subject/ivity is essentially philosophical and this is the sufficient necessary criterion to distinguish philosophy from the scientific thought and the artistic practice. The paragraph from the preface to *Critique of Political Economy* cited above, let us recall, is Marx's testament that *The German Ideology* should be considered as the crystallisation of Marx's and Engel's critique of philosophy (leading to a science of the species being of humanity). In it he seems to have radicalised instead of abandoned his "scientific humanism" and the exit from philosophy or the transcendence of its auto-fetishism remains the prerequisite of such project.

German criticism has, right up to its latest efforts, never quitted the realm of philosophy. Far from examining its general philosophic premises, the

---

[1] In the German original (available in the Marxist Internet Archive): "Wenn der wirkliche, leibliche, auf der festen wohlgerundeten Erde stehende, alle Naturkräfte aus- und einatmende Mensch seine wirklichen, gegenständlichen Wesenskräfte durch seine Entäußerung als fremde Gegenstände setzt, so ist nicht das Setzen Subjekt; [A*] es ist die Subjektivität gegenständlicher Wesenskräfte, deren Aktion daher auch eine gegenständliche sein muß. Das gegenständliche Wesen wirkt gegenständlich, und es wurde nicht gegenständlich wirken, wenn nicht das Gegenständliche in seinen Wesensbestimmung läge. Es schafft, setzt nun Gegenstände, weil es durch Gegenstände gesetzt ist, weil es von Haus aus Natur ist. In dem Akt des Setzens fällt es also nicht aus seiner „reinen Tätigkeit" in ein Schaffen des Gegenstandes, sondern sein gegenständliches Produkt bestätigt nur seine gegenständliche Tätigkeit, seine Tätigkeit als die Tätigkeit eines gegenständlichen natürlichen Wesens."

whole body of its inquiries has actually sprung from the soil of a definite philosophical system, that of Hegel. (Marx, 1959: "Critique of Hegel's Philosophy in General")

Nature, life, and physicality resurface a few pages further in the text, along with the insistence that materiality ought to determine thought rather than the other way around or else we remain entrapped in philosophy:

> In direct contrast to German philosophy which descends from heaven to earth, here we ascend from earth to heaven. That is to say, we do not set out from what men say, imagine, conceive, nor from men as narrated, thought of, imagined, conceived, in order to arrive at men in the flesh. We set out from real, active men, and on the basis of their real life-process we demonstrate the development of the ideological reflexes and echoes of this life-process. (Marx, 1968: *The German Ideology, Part 1: Feuerbach*)

By the very structure of thought subjectivity as the organising principle of an analysis or a theory induces anthropomorphism or atavistic humanism. Individuation conceived in materialist terms, on the other hand, is determined by matter or its elements to which it inevitably dissolves as we read in the paragraph from *Grundrisse* quoted above. Individuation is praxis of the matter and the individual life form, including human, is its result. It is not a process that could predetermine the elements or atoms but always their result—the unruliness of the real is the thesis Marx defended since his dissertation on atomism, i.e., the defense of the Epicurean principle of *clinamen* in Greek atomism. The argument is similar to that made by Simondon: forms do not preexist matter and its movement; they are not fixed and separated from matter, or simply "the individual does not preexist individuation" (Simondon, 2007: 12). More importantly, "the notion of form should be replaced by information, which presupposes the existence of a system in a state of metastable equilibrium endowed with the capacity of individuating itself:

information, unlike form, is never a unique term, but rather a signification surging from a disappearance" (Simondon, 2007: 12). The information that forms individuation is subject to continuous change and, therefore, the morphology of the existing material universe is not exhausted.

To speak of post-humanism is still human centered. On the other hand, to advocate Marxian humanism is to advocate a science of a particular form of reality and history, an instance of individuation materially and historically conditioned, which has its own and unique morphology and identity in the last instance. It is one among the many subject matters of scientific inquiry, and to name it "human" is not about anthropomorphism of thought and human-centeredness but rather about identifying in the last instance the object of inquiry as determined by a particular configuration of materiality. I have proposed at the beginning of the book to radicalise the concept by distinguishing it from philosophical post-enlightenment humanism but also by submitting it in the last instance to the (material) real of humanity and have, thus, termed it "non-human." Let us reiterate, materiality or the determining real insofar as materiality is not necessarily living and organic physicality but also synthetic and machinic too—the "information" stems from materiality. From a materialist point of view, the information is determined in the last instance by the real (of the material), which does not change the fact that the transcendental and the real are in a relation of unilaterality. The automaton is indeed a self-enveloped universe, operating on a premise of its self-sufficiency, and it could indeed constitute a universe completely independent from humanity, as David Roden argues in his discussion on technological substantivism (Roden, 2014: 150–165). Nonetheless, the material basis is a prerequisite for its sustenance. And if the physicality (organicity) or materiality and the automaton constitute such irredeemable asymmetry of political power, resulting into an utter holocaust of the physical (including the human animal) used for sustaining the automaton, we end up with a tautological universe of value/sign production based on an annihilating exploitation of all physical.

Still, such dystopian phantasy is utterly naive—the automaton is devoid of volition and, therefore, at a certain point in time, the exploitation and full combustion of the physical will leave it stripped of its material basis. Without it, the automaton of techno-capital will find itself dismantled. The phantasm of techno-capitalist omnipotence is refuted by the reality of the comical mortality of every automaton, symbolised in the image of a useless floppy disc or Comodore 64.

Speaking in terms of Marxian materialism and non-philosophical realism, the identity in the last instance is materially determined. It can mutate but the mutation must be the product of a mediated materiality rather than imposed imprint of some self-standing form detached from the real as material. If the identity in the last instance at issue is "the human," it is treated as any other identity in the last instance, i.e., in its radical finitude rather than in terms of hegemonic expansion. The possible mutations of form are subject to determination in the last instance as material or, more specifically, they are information. Thus, the concept of information in our discussion is materially determined rather than in terms of the transcendental and the immanent, which are categories that can be applied on material and immaterial reality depending on the type of theorisation but cannot serve as determinations in the last instance. Therefore, a non-anthropocentric post-humanism would radicalise the human and construe a discourse of humanity in scientific terms determined and delineated by the finitude of the reality (of humanity). A Marxist analysis and critique of the treatment of the physical in philosophy and capitalism will lead us to identifying the intersecting and commonly produced realities by the humans and the animals.

If the post-human is extension of humanity, then technology is subjectively speaking prosthesis whereas, objectively, it remains a means of production as Marx treats it in his *Grundrisse: Foundation of the Critique of Political Economy*. The tendency to subjectivise technology, to produce mimicry of humanity, is about "philosophical spontaneity" (Laruelle, 2013a: 9–10) to depart from the given of an individual instead of the process of individuation (Simondon, but also Marx in the *Grundrisse*) as a proper materialist point of departure. A post-philosophical and radically non-humanist axiom will permit variations of individuation, morphologically, structurally, and in substance that will be grounded in the physical materiality regardless of whether organically created or synthetically produced. The possibility of forms, physically speaking, which also includes cognitive consequences, is not exhausted with variations of human form. In line with the same method, radical humanism submits to the materialist determination of the identity in the last instance without transforming it into an ontology, without the philosophical gesture of grounding reality and the real itself but rather correlating with the real. It views humanity in its unilaterality or in terms of the finitude of its determination in the last instance; it is subject to a Vision-in-One as Laruelle would put it (Laruelle, 2013a). Thus, the extension or mutation of technology into ontology—or of *thechné* into *tò ôn*—is a philosophisation of the question, whereas what we propose is a non-philosophical treatment of the technological reality or rather one of a science based on non-philosophy and on Marx's own writings. As already expounded, the scientific treatment of philosophical material—including considerations of technology—can find its model in structuralist linguistic or other methods of more elaborate formalisations of categories derived from philosophy such as psychoanalysis. The ontologisation leads to inevitable subjectivisation as the place philosophy always already arrives at, as Marx explained. Hegel is but the climax of all that is immanently philosophical, writes Marx, and so subjectivism in Hegel as criticised by Marx is what each or all philosophy inevitably amounts to. Therefore, that detached abstraction presuming to constitute a self-sufficient reality called the subject is the mode and posture of thought that is essentially philosophical as well as essentially capitalist as it is worth or value in its purest form, as a self-standing and self-sufficient universe, fully dematerialised.

> The self-abstracted entity, fixed for itself, is man as *abstract egoist—egoism* raised in its pure abstraction to the level of thought. (Marx, 1959: "Critique of Hegel's Philosophy in General")[2]

It is with the posture of thought of the "abstract egoist" that one could envisage "human rights" for the robots or the artificial intelligence (AI) while the possibility of non-subjectivation is not even considered. The "self-abstracted" entity called the human, post-human, or transhuman is the philosophical spontaneous foundation of technological ontology. In that ontology the limits and the form of the universe are those of the subject. Therefore, all practical philosophy, ethics and politics, is framed in terms of subjectivisation or individual rights: "should the robots have human rights?," regardless of whether the robots are utterly indifferent to that question as the real is to the transcendental. Instead, one must ask if we can speak of subjecivisation and subjectivity, and also of individuality and collectivity, and, finally, of rights. Rights to what? To "dignity," "respect of individual choice" or "identity"? Or right to life? If one can speak of life of robots, then perhaps one can speak of rights to life as well. Still, prelingual or postlingual entities, robots and animals equally, are perhaps best protected in terms of defense of their physicality and right to life (which also makes the absence of pain relevant) rather than rights that would emulate abstractions of humanism such as dignity, individuality, identity, etc.

Philosophical impoverishment or a move toward formalisation/universalisation of the categories "nature" and "rights"?

Anthony Paul Smith explains that although the idea of "nature" serves as a limit or conditioning exteriority of philosophical reason, it is nonetheless

---

[2] In the German original available in the online Marxist Internet Archive: "Das für sich abstrahierte und fixierte Selbst ist der Mensch als abstrakter Egoist, der in seine reine Abstraktion zum Denken erhobne Egoismus" (Karl Marx and F. Engels (1967), *Werke, Ergänzungsband, 1. Teil*, Berlin: Dietz Verlag.

product of that same reason (2013: 14–15). That is why the notion of nature should be radicalised by identifying it in the last instance as the clone determined by a singular and unilateral real. It is reducible to physicality but as physical reality can also be artificially produced and sustained, i.e., through human intervention and technology as means of production, whereas nature is the opposite to that, the identity in the last instance needs to be centered on the opposition in question. In order to divest nature of its philosophical representation with the goal of arriving at its non-philosophical definition, we will have to circumvent the trajectory of the "principle of sufficient philosophy" (or *PSP*) and clone the real that determines the notion. Laruelle calls the clone a "description" guided by the syntax of the real—we have elaborated this procedure at length in the preceding chapters, in particular in Chapter 2—and in our case the operation of "cloning" will probably be about marking the trace (coding, inscribing signs) of the structure of a physicality that is *not* produced and maintained via the means of human *techné*. Although such definition is never entirely unambiguous as it relies on an exclusion and, therefore, negation, it will serve as the description that is determined by the real and as an identity of the last instance. We could radicalise or simplify it further in order to arrive at a greater level of formality—in nature, staying in life is autonomous process, an automaton independent from technological intervention even if or when aided by it. Thus, even though the "prime mover" may be a technology, the automaton of life persists on its own.

This automaton is embedded in the material, it is a material process as a matter of fact, and information is part of it as Simondon argued. Life is, therefore, the material process of automated self-preservation guided by something we would call, in a lack of better term, Spinozian *conatus*. The tendency to reduce pain and, instead, increase pleasure issues from the *conatus* itself as Spinoza argued (Spinoza *E III* 29p, 30, 30p). Reducing it in the others concerns the individual not only altruistically but also egotistically: the suffering of the others enters the image of reality and affects (reduces) the level of pleasure in the individual (*E III*, 30p). It leads us to a realisation that Spinoza has applied the method Marx favored centuries later, one we discussed earlier in this chapter (and in the previous chapters)—the perspective of a "third party," whereby the binary of subjective/objective becomes obsolete. *Conatus* is an identity in the last instance, which is determined by the material reality of *life* or it is sublated by the notion of *life*. Therefore, it cannot serve as its determination in the last instance, and the question of divesting the category (of life) from romantic philosophical projections remains unanswered. Instead of following the theological trajectory proposed by Spinoza, let us take a detour and return to the materiality (of life) and its adequate clone or minimal yet fully exhaustive *description*.

The Maßstab (in Wittgenstein's sense discussed previously) of life is found in the processes of becoming individual, staying in life as such and then disintegrating as individual into elemental materiality and in the fact that this automated process is sustained without human intervention. The latter, as already noted, can occur and such occurrence can be a variable in the self-sustained circuit of life. Such automaton is, therefore, in a defining way distinct from the transcendental inventions of humanity including the automaton of capital and its pretentious aspirations that technology or its means of production can constitute a self-standing reality, ideally without any physicality regardless of whether natural or artificial, whether living or not. As already explained, in capitalism, matter is "mere material" to value production and its disappearance enables full value.

A complete holocaust of materiality will amount to the rule of the Absolute Spirit of Capital creating a dead universe and also static—M-M' tautology amounts to motionless affirmation of an abstract identity of Value in and for itself. Therefore, the Maßstab and the clone of "nature" are determined by the automaton of material reality unaided by human intervention in the last instance (save as a variable). The automaton of material reality of nature seems to be identical in the last instance to the "philosophically impoverished" description (Laruelle, 2014: 2) we gave of life as materially determined or, as Laruelle would put it, that is how we *cloned* it. In case of "life" human or technological intervention—or more precisely, capitalo-philosophical intervention—is also to be treated as a variable instead of a determination in the last instance. Formally speaking, and in the context of the presented post-philosophical discussion of radicalised metaphysics of socialism, concerning the reversal of the positions of the physical and the "idea"/"reason," and its political economy, the categories of life and physicality (even if biologically non-living) are interchangeable and can be treated as the same. The living organisms are determined by the ratio of elements that can be found in the non-living physical world such as carbon, hydrogen, and oxygen as well as of proteins and other molecular compounds.

"Rights" are in their last instance determined by the reality of language. The material fact of the ability to use language and thus place a claim to a certain kind of treatment by institutions and states is the determination in the last instance. A claim to something or someone that does not issue from appetite (in Spinozian sense), but is founded on a justification, entails the ability to elaborate it mentally and to enunciate it by use of language, is what determines "right" in legal and political sense. If we are to elaborate "rights" for prelingual or postlingual entities, i.e., for animals and robots respectively, we must resort to post-philosophical discursive possibilities that take us beyond the concept of "rights" as humanist invention. A new social contract that abolishes the possibility of exploitation of life for the purposes of creating surplus value is required. It requires an inauguration of a completely new and unprecedented law and ought to rely on a gesture of Schmittian enactment of sovereignty—the introduction of the new law should resemble a "religious miracle" (Schmitt, 1985: 36) or Walter Benjamin's "divine violence." It would have the status of an axiom of a newly postulated world or a world postulated a new, and the logic of "rights" will not be required in order to provide justification for an effective right.

> But if the existence of violence outside the law, as pure immediate violence, is assured, this furnishes the proof that revolutionary violence, the highest manifestation of unalloyed violence by man, is possible [...] Divine violence, which is the sign and seal but never the means of sacred execution, may be called sovereign violence. (Benjamin, 1999: 300)

A new horizon is needed in which "the right to life" is not discursively negotiated, in which it is not a question of legality but rather a question of sovereign violence that is "the sign and the seal" of a law that will insure it. For such primitive lawmaking to take place, one that stems from the ruins of a previous world, one born as if ex nihilo and out of the substance of divine violence, a revolution is prerequisite. I will argue that revolution is never in singular but rather a multiplicity of acts: they can all be determined in the last instance by the materiality consisted of the revolt of the suffering bodies in conditions of capitalism and by the types of exploitation specific of the suffering. They can all be moved by the same goal, such as establishing a socialist society whose material determination in the last instance would be the abolition of surplus value, but they do not have to be a totality of operations of instilling a predetermined system. The concepts and strategies of lawmaking and institution-building can be born and can develop in different variants depending on different situations. It can be a multiplicity of unilaterally determined realities, moved by numerous instantiations of the same material determination in the last instance, that of establishing a socialist world defined by the absence of surplus value.

The precondition for such order is the "right" to life that is pre-legal and yet again law enabling: the establishment of the new social contract relies on the axiom according to which value is materially determined and is thus non-alienated from physicality and without the tendency to subjugate and exploit it for the production of "value." Thus not merely surplus value but value *tout court*. According to the socialist utopia we are sketching out here, the loss of physical life for the sake of use is determined as life-preserving and should, therefore, regain its sacral status. If such loss is necessary, its transformation on the transcendental plane is required and should be one of sublimation and sacralisation. Considering that it is a matter of culture and technology, we have to conclude that signification and, therefore, value in some utterly new form are produced. What makes that production non-capitalist is that it is not intended for surplus value but also that value is not a self-standing entity and, finally, that the exploited body is not commodified—it is not abstracted and then its value is not fetishised as money and the symbolisms it can afford. As we know from Benjamin and Agamben, sacralisation is enacted in a state of exception when the laws are suspended (Agamben, 2005: 24). Therefore, in a socialist political economy and according to its metaphysics, physicality, and in particular that which is living, is not exploited but its sacrifice is possible under the condition of state of exception only and in the name of use value that is "life increasing." Objectivisation as commodification through abstraction detached from and hostile to physicality or materiality is an utterly different metaphysical stance and ontology enabling both economies, capitalism and philosophy. Sacralisation of life lost in the name of preservation of life takes place under the condition of state of exception and cannot, therefore, be transformed into an industry and object of monetary exchange. The principle law, one that acts as the axiom for the legislation and institutionalisation of the new socialist order, continues to posit that exploitation of life and materiality in the name of surplus value is impermissible as essentially capitalist and contradictory to the socialist utopia.

Holocaust is originally a sacrificial burning of animal flesh. In Greek religion, the sacrifice of animals was always the task of men, priests or not, and this holy sacrificial rite was called *hiereia* or *holocaustos*. Women were, on the other hand, in charge of the sacrifices to the chthonic deities and the dead that never included flesh but rather consisted of grains, liquid offerings such as wine and water or honey, but also dried fruits (Alexiou, 2002: 9–10, 16, 32; Mouliner,

1950: 209, 210, 73, 111, 80–81, 109). The *hiereia*, or the sacrificial ritual dedicated to the life-preserving deities, to the light and reason the Olympians represented, entailed *holocaustos*—burning of the dead animal. Unlike the *enagismata*, the *hiereia* or the *holocaustos* is pure and purifying, the foundation of *logos* and law and order in the polis. The destruction of the physical body ensures immortal light of reason. The complete holocaust of all animal life will insure the complete rule of pure reason or of the Absolute Spirit—the perfect form of capitalism-as-philosophy. *Hiereia*, however, constituted an exception that helped the *polis* preserve normality and continuity of life: they remain attached to the physical body, matter matters and determines the transcendental product, or the sublimation of the sacrificed burnt body into a higher form of existence, i.e., the transcendental. The rites of *hiereiea* cannot be transformed into "pure value," into an abstracted from the body ethereal value transformed into a signifying chain within which exchange and accumulation of worth may take place. They are determined in the last instance by the flesh subject to holocaust and by the fact that the body of sacrifice is determined by the reality of being in a state of exception rather than part of a massive hyper-production (of surplus value) of fetishised abstraction. A complete holocaust equals competition with the immortal gods, and that is *hubris*—the transgression that invites the tragic fall. An absolute transgression brings about an absolute or irredeemable *hamartia*.

4

Homologies and asymmetries between the automata of capital and patriarchy

Reading the P(hallus)-P(hallus) tautology as the M-M tautology derived from M-C-M

Phallus, as a symbol taken from Lacanian psychoanalysis and Irigaray's declination of it, holds a position similar to that of capital in the market exchange system. Commodities or women-as-femininity—not women as the real as they precede value—are the relay of value or sign communicating with value and sign, a currency of the auto-referentiality according to the equation M-C-M, which always yields in M-M' or simply M-M. The heteronormative chain of signification is perpetual repetition of the automaton P(hallus)-P(hallus) or hom(m)o-sexuality, explains Irigaray in *This Sex Which Is Not One* (1985a). The fetish, or rather commodity, is not a subjectivity or an agency and it does not possess desire, argues Irigaray. Within the capitalist and patriarchal universe of the value exchange automaton or the automaton of signification, hom(m)o-sexuality engenders masculinity and reaffirms it as the only reality. Femininity remains the currency or the general equivalent that enables the endless multitude of the same tautology. Love caught up in the patriarchal-capitalist automaton of signification will remain atavistic regardless of the interventions of technology, which neither guaranty nor imply transcendence of women's status as commodities and resource. Only a political reversal of the underlying automata (of capitalism and patriarchy) can enable change in input for the "post-human" or "non-human" agencies of pleasures and of the trauma called love. Such political reversal cannot avoid coming to grips with the questions of subject and object, physicality and its opposites, the one and the multiple, the real and the fiction and the related binaries insofar as metaphysical rather than philosophical in their determinations in the last instance.

> In still other words: all the systems of exchange that organize patriarchal societies and all the modalities of productive work that are recognized, valued, and rewarded in these societies are men's business. The production of women, signs, and commodities is always referred back to men (when a man buys a girl, he "pays" the father or the brother, not the mother …), and they always pass from one man to another, from one group of men to another. The work force is thus always assumed to be masculine and "products" are objects to be used, objects of transaction among men alone. Which means that the possibility of our social life, of our culture, depends upon a ho(m)mo-sexual monopoly? The law that orders our society is the exclusive valorization of men's needs/desires, of exchanges among men. What the anthropologist calls the passage from nature to culture thus amounts to the institution of the reign of hom(m)o-sexuality. Not in an "immediate" practice, but in its "social" mediation. From this point on, patriarchal societies might be interpreted as societies functioning in the mode of "semblance. (Irigaray, 1985a: 171)

In her book *This Sex Which Is Not One* (1985a), Irigaray makes a claim as grandiose as the one in *Speculum* (1985b) in which she reduces Western philosophical reason to speculative masculinity as ideologised form of cognition, by stating that "passage from nature to culture thus amounts to the institution of the reign of hom(m)o-sexuality" (171). Hom(m)o-sexuality is not to be understood as homosexuality either among men or women. The concept has nothing to do with the question of sexual orientation or gender identity. Sexual practice and identity are in fact irrelevant in this conceptualisation: hom(m)osexuality refers to the auto-generation of the "human" occupied by the male and fetishised as masculinity. Its philosophical determination is underpinned by masculinism as "the production of values and signs" has always been the trade of and among men, argues Irigaray (1985a: 171). That production is carried out on the basis of holocaust of materiality, physicality, animality, and femininity antecedent to fetishisation.

> In this new matrix of History, in which man begets man as his own likeness, wives, daughters, and sisters have value only in that they serve as the possibility of, and potential benefit in, relations among men. The use of and traffic in women subtend and uphold the reign of masculine hom(m)o-sexuality, even while they maintain that hom(m)o-sexuality in speculations, mirror games, identifications, and more or less rivalrous appropriations, which defer its real practice. (Irigaray, 1985a: 171–172)

What is exchanged in patriarchy is not merely women as use value for reproduction but also femininity or fetishised femaleness as surplus value. The pure value, femininity as abstracted and dematerialised femaleness, is exchanged in the same way as commodity adding value to the tautology of exchanging the same for the same: M-M or P-P in order to achieve M-M' or P-P'. The structuralist analysis proffered by Claude Lévi-Strauss divulges the reality of patriarchy as value/signifier exchange system: women are currency whereas what is maintained and grows is cultural form of sexual reproduction—patriarchy.

> Exchange, as a total phenomenon, is from the first a total exchange, comprising food, manufactured objects, and that most precious category of goods, women. (Lévi-Strauss, 1969: 60–61)

Patriarchal family is the only form of family humanity has ever known, regardless of whether patrilineal or matrilineal. (Kinship is more physical, not necessarily biological but nonetheless physically immediate.) The exchange serves not only to increase and enforce the capital of masculinity but also to add sheer surplus value to it, an excess in value (not libido) as a marker of erected phallic power. The power seen not as materiality but as value is a set of signifiers: a patriarch, the guardian of the household or *oikos*, individual and collective or of *oikos* and the *oikonomia* of a state (or any form of organised community), and potent reproducer of the same—*homo* as *homoios* (in Greek) but also *homo* (in Latin) and its derivations like *l'homme* (French), or the human as male. Family is hom(m)osexual by its inherent laws, i.e., it is patriarchal—there is no form of family that could subvert this norm as its material determination in the last instance is the signifying automaton of patriarchy. Post-humanist forms of kinship should place themselves beyond human morphology and its residuals such as fetishisations of maleness and femaleness and their variations. "Sexual identities" equal commodity in the overall automaton of hom(m)o-sexual identification—they are fetish par excellence.

Again, post-humanist discourse rid of philosophical sufficiency should radicalise the human-technology dyad instead of expand or accelerate the post-human as transhuman. Bringing sexual practices back to their use value is not about bringing them to reproduction (as that would be reducing it to family creation) but to the realness of sexuality whose materiality in the last instance is determined by the physical pleasure.

In the case of submitting to the determination in the last instance of use value rather than surplus value, the fetish, which is perhaps a defining element of sexual pleasure as material experience, does not undergo full dematerialisation or commodification. Femaleness becomes gapingly real; the woman becomes the Medusa of the bizarre mélange of birth and death and blood and an engulfing uterus (Vernant, 1995). Femininity serves not only for transformation of (reproductive) use value into surplus value or simply value but also to erase the Medusa-like inhumanity of femaleness. It, therefore, purports to be self-sufficient just as the truth in the automaton of philosophy and the monetary value in the capitalist automaton. Gendered identity serves to erase the unruly real of physicality (not only sexual, but in general: for example, a gentleman, pater familias, a master not merely a man, etc.)

As Plato explains in *Timaeus*, male sperm should not be seen as matter as it is *nous* or reason (because intentionality consisting in it being the active aspect) whereas woman, seen as the recipient, is reduced to passivity and materiality. Thus, woman or matter as such (including sperm), is the relay of *homo* (as man or l'homme) reproducing himself. Just as we can expunge C(ommodity) from the M-C-M formula, we can also expunge F(emininity) from the P(hallus)-F(emininity)-P(hallus) formula and conclude that patriarchy is best explained through the tautological formula P-P. Passivity as devoid of agency is what defines matter from the standpoint of speculative reason or reason philosophical, capitalist, and patriarchal. Agency is a form of subjectivity or an abstraction of the human self. All that is bereft of subjectivity is matter and also passive, and its only validation can be transformation into value, meaning or purpose—an entity of the transcendental, in its substance to be likened or correspond in some sense to "subjectivity." In order for this transformation to come about, a *holokaustos* of the flesh and other forms of the material must take place, ritually and literally. It serves the phantasm of the Spartans: they are unborn, without ever having been borne in woman's womb; they are created out of sperm only; and they are warriors. Athena is also born from her father's head or she is the product of *nous* or reason and wisdom that could only be masculine. She is not only the goddess of rational wisdom but also of war. The sperm that gave birth to the Spartans or Zeus's head is practically non-physical or minimally physical and in being such it is purely masculine. In other words, the transcendence of physicality of the male reproductive role equals masculinity. Femininity is reified; it is fetishised and, therefore, commodified flesh.

Such would be the perfect human, the semblance of God or the gods, yet still imperfect and mortal due to their being flesh, animal-like susceptible to decay as all matter is. The eternal truths, including the Being as unity of the real and truth resulting into sublation of the real, are unchanging because they are by definition perfect—a-temporality, immobility, and absolute stability are the characteristics of the Transcendental, of signification or meaning and truth. The automaton is perfect and errors can appear only due to mortal or physical imperfection: human or hardware error. Thus, the erasing of flesh is about erasing decay, temporality, and history. Same goes for other forms of materiality. Woman with her bleeding genitalia, painful giving childbirth, deformed pregnant, and breastfeeding body is too reminiscent of the animal. Femaleness along with the animal ought to be erased for the pure value to take their place. In the contemporary world run by the Automaton-of-Capital, the highest form of derealisation (as dematerialisation) of value or the one of strongest effect of political power is that of finance: it subordinates the other automata that feed into it and create a spiral of automata around the axis of capital. There is no surprise then that in the *Communist Manifesto* Marx and Engels insist that a true communist society is predicated on the abolishment of marriage as social and political-economic form "reducing women to an instrument of production" (1969b: 25).

Erasing the traces of the female animal or female as animal through fetishisation

The same metaphysics, that of speculative reason or of the principle of philosophical sufficiency, rules the automata around the axis of capital. It is the metaphysics of the "holocaust of the animal" that underpins the logic of the automaton of sufficient philosophy, capitalism, and patriarchy, and it is not an easy task to establish, which is more primordial. Diachronically speaking, patriarchy comes first and predetermines the other automata of the same axis. That is why I find the following quote from Marx so telling:

> In simple circulation, C-M-C, the value of commodities attained at the most a form independent of their use-values, i.e., the form of money; but that same value now in the circulation M-C-M, or the circulation of capital, suddenly presents itself as an independent substance, endowed with a motion of its own, passing through a life-process of its own, in which money and commodities are mere forms which it assumes and casts off in turn. Nay, more: instead of simply representing the relations of commodities, it enters now, so to say, into private relations with itself. It differentiates itself as original value from itself as surplus-value; as the father differentiates himself from himself qua the son, yet both are one and of one age: for only by the surplus-value of £10 does the £100 originally advanced become capital, and so soon as this takes place, so soon as the son, and by the son, the father, is begotten, so soon does their difference vanish, and they again become one. (Karl Marx, *Capital*, Vol. I, Part 2, Chapter 4)

The metaphor of the father being begotten by the son is a literal description of the surplus value production in the automaton of patriarchy. "The son," or P', is in fact what makes the physical father a P, analogous to the M in the M-C-M formula, and more than use value in sexual reproduction—it is transformed into "symbolic capital" (although capital is always symbolic) or assumes the phallic position precisely through its replication or tautological reaffirmation in the form of the son. Unless the trade of females either through marriage or through an actual industry of sexual reproduction is abolished, patriarchy as capitalist automaton will perpetuate itself.

The circular tautological movement elides the physical female and, thus, Phallus engenders Phallus, whereas the fetish of femininity is an excess of surplus value that pretends to be self-sufficient, a specular entity of the Transcendental enabled by the *holocaust* of its physicality. In the capitalist world, the excess of commodity production is solved through holocaust of use value—literal destruction of products—in order to preserve the mathematical projection of surplus value. The physical body is material of identity recreation and its purpose (as its *causa finalis*) is its own full holocaust—as with all materiality—in order to produce the fetish-based surplus value as the only form of value that enters the automaton of patriarchy-capital. As the fetish is fully abstracted to the extent of evacuating relevance of any physicality—similarly to Marx's explanation that the automaton of capital will eliminate not only commodity but money as fetish recognising the irrelevance of materiality—so does the P-P' continue in perpetuity without the need of actual women (except as receptacles, as in Plato's *Timaeus*), not even in their fetishised form. Gender as dematerialised abstraction—as understood in terms of identity politics—is mere commodity P-P' can do without. Coexistence of different sexualities, conceived in their materiality, with the automaton of P-P', is nothing other than complicity with the patronising patriarchy of the post-neoliberal era. To aspire for equality in marriage and in relation to the two normative genders is to participate in the pacification of the subversive force of sexual queerness and the possibility of feminist Marxism.

The first condition for the appearance of the cyborg, Haraway argues, is the hybridisation of the animal and technology, resulting into "bestiality" as its underpinning quality (Haraway, 1991: 152). On previous pages of this book we discuss the concept of the radical dyad and take Haraway's notion of the cyborg as the exemplar of the technology-body dyad the human is identified as in his/her/their last instance. The body in Haraway is the identifier for animality as one element of the dyad whereas technology appears to be an externality that is nonetheless in hybridised continuity with the animal aspect. The continuity is not conceptual: it is material, whereas on transcendental level there is discontinuity, which is grounding and unsurpassable (and without the need to be surpassed). In her preface to the *Cyborg Handbook* edited by Chris Hables Gray, Haraway explains that the humans have always been post-human or in fact cyborgs (Haraway, 1995: xi–xx). What makes us cyborgs is the mere extension of the tool. Considering language is an artifice, an automaton of signification, we could say that our signifying capacity, or ability to create the plane of the transcendental, is what makes us cyborgs or constitutes us as the radical dyad explained in the opening pages of this book. That dyad is messy, does not amount to some superior truth, and does not entail any process of sublation: it is inhuman or it is Cthulhu, explains Haraway in her 2016 article for E-flux. In her Cyborg manifesto, she calls this continuity "bestial":

> And many people no longer feel the need for such a separation; indeed, many branches of feminist culture affirm the pleasure of connection of human and other living creatures. Movements for animal rights are not irrational denials of human uniqueness; they are a clear-sighted recognition of connection across the discredited breach of nature and culture. The cyborg appears in myth precisely where the boundary between human and animal is transgressed. Far from signalling a walling off of people from other living beings, cyborgs signal distrurbingly and pleasurably tight coupling. Bestiality has a new status in this cycle of marriage exchange. (Haraway, 1991: 152)

As already argued, marriage exchange amounts to surplus value of phallic power or masculinity. The figure of the warrior is maintained by a holocaust of animality and femininity and it is the basis of the exchange of the pure value of patriarchy. The same preconditions are required for the maintenance of the automata of philosophy and speculative or capitalist economy. An intervention that is both categorical (of the transcendental) and material (of the real) that rearranges the boundaries can destablise and possibly founder the marriage exchange automaton:

> Monsters have always defined the limits of community in Western imaginations. The Centaurs and Amazons of ancient Greece established the limits of the centred polls of the Greek male human by their disruption of marriage and boundary pollutions of the warrior with animality and woman. (Haraway, 1991: 177)

Haraway's cyborg is not a figure of perfection, it is not a perfectly humanoid machine, and it is not about flawless accuracy and potency. Quite the contrary: it is fragile, vulnerable; it is about pollution and disruption; it is bestial or monstrously animal-like. It is also a feminist figure because it not only disrupts but ultimately demolishes the "marriage exchange" (be it of women or men—marriage *tout court*) as the automaton of P-P'. As argued above, in line with Marx's commitment to abolishment of bourgeois marriage and Irigaray's equation of the automaton of patriarchy with that of capital, let us note that the exchange of women, but also marriage exchange (which always involves exploitation of female bodies even if not between men and women), has political-economic consequences. The transformation of *oikos* is the precondition for an economic transformation and for the establishment of a post-capitalist or socialist *oikonomia*. Haraway's cyborg takes on this mission and it is feminist insofar as it deals with the transformation of the *oikonomia* (economy) that is currently maintained through exploitation of female bodies. It is about class, economy, and feminism without addressing the issues of gender and sexuality as identity or, simply, without addressing them at all (regardless of whether treated as identity or possibly in terms of materialism).

No longer structured by the polarity of public and private, the cyborg defines a technological polls based partly on a revolution of social relations in the oikos, the household. Nature and culture are reworked; the one can no longer be the resource for appropriation or incorporation by the other. (Haraway, 1991: 150)

The cyborg, the feminist and socialist "post-human" we call inhuman or non-human, is about reworking the nature-culture relation in such a way that none can longer be the "resource for appropriation or incorporation by the other": nature can no longer be mere resource for exploitation for the purposes of producing pure (monetary) value. Moreover, technology (or culture) cannot and should not "incorporate" the body nor the other way around. The body cannot be the material for the perfect automaton regardless of whether technological, political-economic, or patriarchal. In other words, "culture" and "nature" (or the automaton of signification and the physical) constitute a Laruellian radical dyad: they establish an inextricably material unity while being unilaterally positioned toward one another. The consequence of such unilateral positioning is that there is no mediation or unification via the transcendental—one of the two elements of the dyad plays the role of the real to the other. The continuity is sheer materiality and it also performs the function of exteriority or the real vis-à-vis the signifying automaton.

The Indispensable alienation for the species being of humanity and its erasure via philosophical alienation

The sense of alienation, the sense of an "I" that does not fully experience itself as unity or an "I," is the creation of the philosophical determination of the signifying automaton of the capitalist era. The automaton aspires to occupy and unify that territory of the inhuman as the transcendental seeks to use up and efface the physical. It nonetheless remains embarrassingly attached to "the self" and even more embarrassingly when the self is no more than a subject or mere effect of the automaton. The transhumanist and post-structuralist project centered on the notion of the subject and the spectral entities called "identities" seeks to fully appropriate the natural and transform it into mere resource. Such tendency is incompatible with either Marx or the feminist Marxism of Irigaray and Haraway. The drama of alienation and the ambition to heal it are the product of philosophical pretentiousness. The socialist, however, knows the individual and collective human to be non-human (in the non-philosophical sense)—it is an unruly compound whose material continuity provides a physical sense of unity whereas the dyad is recognised on transcendental level. The non-human has a single identity in the last instance, that of the radical dyad, whereas the automaton establishes an affinity with the animal generating material unity or the real of continuity the dyad is made of. Within the real of the body or the real of the automaton (as it is endowed with its own material reality) is an exteriority that disturbs the sense of unity experienced by what we will call here radical subjectivity. That primordial estrangement, which is integral to the sense of material continuity, is what moves the species being of humanity as an *oikonomia*.

In *Théorie des Etrangers: Science des hommes, démocratie et non-psychanalyse* (1995), referred to here as "Theory of the Strangers," Laruelle elaborates the notion of the Stranger or radical subjectivity. He subjects Lacan's psychoanalysis to a non-philosophical or non-Euclidian angle of operation radicalising the repository of concepts, postulates, and methods, by stripping them of their philosophical sufficiency. The subject is an effect of the signifying automaton as Lacan insists, but it is also an instance that imitates the form of the human and executes the role of the "I" or the "Self." Such elevation of the subject to the level of philosophical projection of the human is always already failed as the subject is indeed an effect of the signifying automaton and, therefore, remains a certain exteriority inside the "human-in-human" (Laruelle, 1995: 166). It is an exteriority to the human-in-human that is in the last instance determined by the real of the lived as unreflected experience: it is lived without being shaped and given meaning by a truth called life; it is lived without life or it is "le joui sans jouissance" (Laruelle, 1995: 87). This lived without life is the reality of experience without the philosophical procedure of transforming the material given (of life or of living) into life-as-meaning.

The latter is yet another example of philosophical amphibology whereby "the mere physicality" of life is transformed into a meaning that is overdetermined by—and also overdetermining of—life. In other words, it is the parameter according to which one decides which life is worth living or, even more precisely, grieving and which one isn't (Butler, 2006: 30–36). The search of the meaning of life and the decision what that meaning is can determine if an instance of life is worth preserving or dispensing with. The capitalist method in such procedure would be to make sure that life is not dispensed senselessly—as, say, a potlach or any other non-invested expenditure—or without a purpose and gain, i.e., without producing a value. In fact, "meaning of life" is synonymous with *value* of life. The question of life worth living and grieving, as Judith Butler would put it (Butler, 2004: 27; 2006: 36), is a question of political economy and, as a consequence, of modern philosophy. It is precisely in the habitual modern treatment of life—or of the material reality of the "lived" (*le vécu*) as human life—that one witnesses the philosophical operation par excellence: the decision as to whether a real *is* or *is not*, literally so, but also in the sense of valuation. In fact, the procedure of valuation enables the decision of whether something *is* (human life or life worth living) and, therefore, whether it *should be*. It can easily lead to dispensing with it completely albeit while frugally investing it into a process that can produce value. A "post-vitalist" or non-vitalist post-humanist treatment of life would transform it into mere material of value production. Life worth living is life "with a purpose," "life that makes sense," "life invested into a meaning." The mere fact of life bereft of meaning is brute materiality or physicality that is supposed to be subjected to cleverly invested holocaust. That kind of life is lived without life or *le vécu*.

The lived (*le vécu*) ought to be mediated via the transcendental, argues Laruelle, in his *Theory of the Strangers* (1995). Communication is an artifice and it is necessary that the automaton of signification clones the non-human or signifies the unity (without unification) or the material continuity of the self. The "estrangement" thus produced is grounded in material continuity. That originary estrangement that occurs on the terrain of the prelingual yet constituting language is grounded in the real, and, in Laruelle, that form of "radical subjectivity" is called "the Stranger." The signifying automaton and the subject as its product (or effect) do not take themselves to be self-standing realities nor to constitute a reality more perfect than the "mere real" that hasn't been endowed with meaning and elevated into truth. Speaking from a non-philosophical or post-philosophical perspective, they are the artifice that is an extension of the human-in-human. That is why "they" do not experience a sense of alienation or "they" do not produce such experience in the non-human—they are not determined by philosophical sufficiency and, therefore, the non-human does not take them to be the "true self." Nor the other way around: the non-human or the radical subjectivity does not take the body or the prelingual lived to be *unheimlich* as its determination in the last instance is not philosophy and its principle of sufficiency. It does not expect any unification into a truth, one that would transcend the messiness of physicality, but rather finds itself at home in the real that precedes language, in the body, in the familiar exteriority, and in the intimate experience that lacks language while nonetheless invites it. At this point stems Laruelle's radical subjectivity or the Stranger.

Marx, on the other hand, writes of a procedure of thought defining of philosophy that consists in estranging the originary and unavoidable estrangement by transforming it into an "as if a thing" albeit not real, a reified abstraction. Later in *Capital* Marx describes identical procedure in the creation of the capitalist fetish or the institution of money and commodities as abstractions turned things—the gesture of reification or *Verdinglichung*. The human subject or the "self-consciousness," a mental activity of the self, turned into a thing or a self-standing real is the philosophical and, evidently, the capitalist self and it is the product of reification.

> And since it is not real man, nor therefore nature—man being human nature—who as such is made the subject, but only the abstraction of man—self-consciousness—thinghood [*Dingheit*] cannot be anything but alienated self-consciousness. It is only to be expected that a living, natural being equipped and endowed with objective (i.e., material) essential powers should have real natural objects of his essence; and that his self-alienation should lead to the positing of a real, objective world, but within the framework of externality, and, therefore, an overwhelming world not belonging to his own essential being. There is nothing incomprehensible or mysterious in this. It would be mysterious, rather, if it were otherwise. (Marx, 1959: "Critique of Hegel's Philosophy in General")

The primordial and founding estrangement that is in material continuity with the body and the prelingual self is familiar. The sense of familiarity is ensured through the material continuity explained above. Moreover, the originary and necessary estrangement is the source of human productivity and of the creation of the universe of social relations; it is at the heart if not the beating heart of the species being of humanity and in being such it creates an objective or "external world": "his self-alienation should lead to the positing of a real, objective world, but within the framework of externality, and, therefore, an overwhelming world not belonging to his own essential being" (Marx, 1959). Instead of subjectivising its capacity of abstraction, instead of anthropomorphising it by creating a homology of the human form, the non-human self (or post-human without philosophy) practices abstraction in order to create a material world. The world of art and artifice, the world of machine and the world of sciences, the reality of social relations are in continuity with nature and stem from and remain grounded in the physical reality.

Philosophy, conversely, engulfs practice and exteriority too into its constitution of the human subjectivity or Subjectivity *tout court*, into the abstracted and generalised abstraction (like in the example of Hegel's Absolute Spirit) purporting to be a fully realised reality. The abstraction of the self—the practice of self-consciousness or reflexivity of cognition—institutes itself not only at the center of the universe as its sole form but also (and even more so) as the universe itself. Therefore, the world in Laruellian sense, i.e., the world as philosophy, or the world of social relations in Marxian sense, i.e., social relations as real abstractions (rather than reifications), takes the form of the Universal Egoist.

> The self-abstracted entity, fixed for itself, is man as abstract egoist—egoism raised in its pure abstraction to the level of thought. (Marx, 1959: "Critique of Hegel's Philosophy in General")

The fixation on issues that would establish a perfect equation between truth and the world, or the real as traumatically estranged outsideness to the thinking subject that is sublated through unification in transcendence, is the symptom of the "Universal Egoist." This is the determination in the last instance of philosophical reason and also of world as philosophy, according to Laruelle (as we have explained on previous pages of this book). The human subject of the capitalist automaton, produced as an effect of the signifying chain and then morphed into the form-of-Human (of Enlightenment or of Western rationalism), is predicated on the same dialectics between truth (or abstraction) and the real (or physicality). The self is reduced to a subject, a signifying effect, whereas materiality is treated as mere resource to the production of the subject or the self as pure value, i.e., an agency of "rights."

Haraway, conversely, affirms the founding hybridity or the radical dyad—the asymmetric, messy, and inhuman core of the human self is affirmed rather than neatly folded and erected into pure and spectral Value (a Subject-of-rights). Technology is in prosthetic continuity with the animal self as not just a body but a sense of self endowed with sensations such as affinity or pleasure (Haraway, 1991: 150). It does not sublate the physical in order to arrive at pure reason, logic, and rationality. Quite the opposite, the physical and/or the animal is empowered through technology as its extension or *prosthesis*. Nonetheless the inhuman or the cyborg is not reducible to any of the aspects of the dichotomy: in the last instance, it is neither machine nor animal. The "bestial cyborg" is the monster of the two, an irrevocable dichotomy or rather an irredeemable dyad.

The xeno-feminist project: A question of its proximity to Marx's affirmation of the first alienation

The xeno-feminist project seems to recognise some of the political and economic potential in the naive metaphysics of the originary alienation. It is naive in the sense that it is proto-philosophical or anterior to any possibility of philosophy, undercutting the philosophical possibility by assuming the stance of science or art. The Laboria Cuboniks collective seems to operate with the notion of "alienation" in a philosophically spontaneous way, but it nonetheless works beyond or outside philosophy due to the pre-philosophical metaphysics of the notion to which the xeno-feminist project resorts in the first instance. Still, it seems that rationality and rationalism are equated with scientific reason in the project at issue. Nonetheless, as we have previously demonstrated, they are not the same thing according to their determination in the last instance. We have demonstrated on the previous pages of this book that "rationalism" is a philosophical precept or a projection containing ontology as much as it contains epistemology but also practical reason (ethics and morality). Scientific reason is indifferent to the values of reason or of rationality. It is indifferent to values. It is an artifice and art, *techné*, put in action in order to produce knowledge about the surrounding reality. Knowledge has practical function in organising the species being of humanity but it also serves the metaphysical function of establishing certain control over the outsideness (Löffler, 2018: 14) as itself a metaphysical category.

As said in the previous chapters, sciences and arts are also moved by metaphysical anxieties that trigger the need of explanation and control. Whereas science and art submit to the real and seek to control it via the proxy of technology, via tool and *metis*, without the pretension to "grasp it in its totality," philosophy seeks to establish absolute certainty by erasing that primordial anxiety caused by the out-there. The latter is the real that has to be supplanted by the pure value of subjectivity, by the absolute of subjectivity or by the pure self—the embarrassing real of the originary estrangement is what philosophy seeks to erase. It is messy and it divulges the constitutive hybridity of the non-human. The xeno-feminist project retains not only the philosophically spontaneous use of the concept of "rationality" but also of "nature" and does not identify the humanist origin of the latter and the philosophical sufficiency of the naturalist mythos. Nature to which reason is opposed is born inside the enlightenment project (and rationalism that immediately precedes it) as a humanist project par excellence. As already said and explained, philosophical humanism is inherently linked with capitalism. In *The Xenofeminist Manifesto*, the dialectics between physicality and the automaton of signification, between matter and idea, between the Absolute (of Pure Reason?) and "nature," remains utterly atavistic, i.e., philosophically humanist.

> XF seizes alienation as an impetus to generate new worlds. We are all alienated—but have we ever been otherwise? It is through, and not despite, our alienated condition that we can free ourselves from the muck of immediacy. Freedom is not a given—and it's certainly not given by anything

"natural." The construction of freedom involves not less but more alienation; alienation is the labour of freedom's construction. Nothing should be accepted as fixed, permanent, or "given"—neither material conditions nor social forms. XF mutates, navigates and probes every horizon. Anyone who's been deemed "unnatural" in the face of reigning biological norms, anyone who's experienced injustices wrought in the name of natural order, will realize that the glorification of 'nature' has nothing to offer us—the queer and trans among us, the differently-abled, as well as those who have suffered discrimination due to pregnancy or duties connected to child-rearing. XF is vehemently anti-naturalist. Essentialist naturalism reeks of theology—the sooner it is exorcised, the better. (Laboria Cuboniks, 2015: 0x01)

The opposition to naturalism remains entrapped in the old humanism as it seems to be determined inside the binary naturalism/rationalism, which is a simple extension of the Cartesian divide. The notion of naturalism obfuscates the devaluation or subordination of matter and physicality to the cognitive practice turned into self-standing abstraction (of the Universal Egoist) or the all-encompassing entity of Reason. Xeno-feminism is, therefore, not so much "vehemently anti-naturalist" as it is anti-materialist. This is one of its two aspects that reveal the project's complicity with capitalism. The other is the absolute absence of any call toward seizing the means of production. In fact, such call is *a priori* disabled by the very fact that, in the framework of this particular philosophical project, technology is subjectivised rather than seen as the externality produced by the originary alienation Marx wrote about. Thus it is not recognised as means of production. No surprise then that the Manifesto calls on negotiating with capitalism for more rights, less consumerism, better protection of vulnerable social groups instead of postulating a completely new and socialist political-economic infrastructure. It makes an indirect plea for "a capitalism with a human face," to paraphrase Žižek, and, if possible, a less patriarchal one.

Why is there so little explicit, organized effort to repurpose technologies for progressive gender political ends? XF seeks to strategically deploy existing technologies to re-engineer the world. Serious risks are built into these tools; they are prone to imbalance, abuse, and exploitation of the weak. Rather than pretending to risk nothing, XF advocates the necessary assembly of techno-political interfaces responsive to these risks. Technology isn't inherently progressive. Its uses are fused with culture in a positive feedback loop that makes linear sequencing, prediction, and absolute caution impossible. Technoscientific innovation must be linked to a collective theoretical and political thinking in which women, queers, and the gender non-conforming play an unparalleled role. (Laboria Cuboniks, 2015: 0x02)

In spite of the potential to be radically disruptive with regard to the automata of capital and patriarchy in place in the twenty-first century, the xenofeminist project does not achieve the set goal due to being determined in the last instance by philosophy (in spite of its science-oriented discourse). It also seems to extend instead of transcending the post-structuralist humanist morphology of genders remaining entrenched in identity politics in spite of the project's universalist commitment. Women, whether trans or biological, suffer a position of society determined by the automaton of patriarchy and the currency of femininity is detached from the use value of either pleasure or reproduction. This is a precondition for the holocaust of not just the female bodies but the bodies of femininity too, intersecting different cultures conditioned and determined in the last instance by global capitalism.

But first, the perennial divide between reason and "emotion," which is often merely sidelined form of reason rather than the opposite of it or a "perfectly reasonable" affective reaction (Power, 2016: 26), and its gendering must be transcended. The divide is the result of the old philosophical-theological somatophobia that has always equated the body or physicality with femaleness, endowing the male human animal with the ability to erect itself to the status of pure subjectivity or pure reason (as self-standing entity). Instead of seeking access to "rationalism," a feminist of the twenty-first century ought to acknowledge the fallacy of the opposition and its atavism, and the fact that it is in utter collision with contemporary cognitive sciences. To conclude, let us consider the following quote by Nina Power:

> But how does rationalism overall fare in the Xenofeminist and gender abolitionist universe? What would a rationalism stripped of its masculinist history look like? I want to claim that this rationalism must also be an emotionalism, that is to say, a neglect of the rational basis for anger, misery, hatred, love, care and so on will likely end up reinstating old oppositions and with them, gendered presuppositions about where thought "belongs" […] Gender is the violence done to both reason and emotion by virtue of separating the two along sexed lines. Philosophy need not be the victim of this. (Power, 2016: 26)

Xeno-feminism, gender abolitionism and other forms of feminist realism that perpetuate the old somatophobia remain complicit with philosophy and its principle of sufficiency. Therefore, they remain archaically humanist or anthropocentric in spite of the opposite intentions. Rationalism must be reinvented by way of assuming scientific or non-philosophical posture of thought: it should correspond with the scientific accounts of what counts as "rationalism" in philosophy by way of "flattening its ontology" or rather stripping it of ontology (and philosophy) entirely. In that way, the masculinist fallacy of the rationalism/emotionalism opposition will be disclosed and a non-philosophical approach (not necessarily Laruellian) can be prompted.

5

New political economy is possible only under the condition of abolishment of the metaphysics of animal-for-killing

The non-human and the non-animal or the human animal without humanism

In an article published in *Angelaki* in 2014, John Ó Maoilearca writes, "Yet the 'animal turn' in recent philosophical thought—much of which now inflates, or restores, the value of the animal—is no less philosomorphic" (Ó Maoilearca, 2014: 121). By "philosomorphic" Ó Maoilearca means anthropomorphic too because humanism is a philosophical creation, embedded in the constitution of philosophy itself and conditioned by it. According to Laruelle, philosophy, insofar as a Greek-Judaic metaphysical invention, is centered on the human self: in Europe as civilisation—or as Gil Anidjar would say "as the only Civilization" (Anidjar, 2014)—theology serves to explain the centrality of the human in considerations of outside reality. The great out-there bends to the shape and the needs of the human subjectivity, and the gods are morphing in line with the diktat of the human self or thought. A non-philosophical or Laruellian turn would be an overhaul of this entire logic, by way of radical democratisation of thought and "flattened ontology" (DeLanda, 2002: 47). The flattening I have in mind is not an ontologisation of some idea of horizontal democracy but is rather evocative Laruelle's use of the method of superposition borrowed from the quantum theory (Gangle and Greve, 2017). This is a thesis Ó Maoilearca fully develops in his later publication *All Thoughts Are Equal* (2015) by way of introducing the notion of the non-human as non-animal (or animal without philosophical humanism). It is upon the extermination of the animal, including the human animal, that man or l'Homme is introduced at the center of the world-as-thought (or philosophy). To institute the real as what succumbs to thought and reflects the narcissistic hallucinations of the human (or rather, man) is to enact the founding principle of philosophy, i.e., the principle of sufficient philosophy (PSP).

As already discussed, the principle of philosophical sufficiency comes down to what Laruelle identified as philosophy's immanent tendency, namely to subjectivise exteriority or to submit the real to the diktat of thought and engage in an amphibology of the two (2013a). Laruelle subscribes to Marx's reading of the problem of philosophy as trapped in its circularity and inability to account of the real or of materiality and practice (2014). Indeed, Marx's critique of philosophy as subject-centered knowledge underpinned by the ambitions of science, namely to explain the real, while always already failing at realising them, is in correspondence with Laruelle's critique of philosophy as defined by the gesture of submitting the real to thought. Moreover, Marx elaborates his method of the third person's perspective with the help of his version of "naturalism," which has nothing to do with vitalism but is rather a form of materialism and realism whereby thought submits to exteriority or reality rather than the other way around:

> Man is directly a natural being. As a natural being and as a living natural being he is on the one hand endowed with natural powers, vital powers—he is an active natural being. These forces exist in him as tendencies and abilities—as instincts. On the other hand, as a natural, corporeal, sensuous objective being *he is a suffering, conditioned and limited creature, like animals and plants.* [my emphasis] That is to say, the objects of his instincts exist outside him, as objects independent of him; yet these objects are objects that he needs—essential objects, indispensable to the manifestation and confirmation of his essential powers. To say that man is a corporeal, living, real, sensuous, objective being full of natural vigour is to say that he has real, sensuous objects as the object of his being or of his life, or that he can only express his life in real, sensuous objects. To be objective, natural and sensuous, and at the same time to have object, nature and sense outside oneself, or oneself to be object, nature and sense for a third party, is one and the same thing. (Marx, 1959: "Critique of Hegel's Philosophy in General")

The reverse form of submission, however, is the reason why philosophy inevitably fails at fulfilling its defining ambition according to Marx, as argued in his *Theses on Feuerbach* and *Critique of Hegel's Philosophy in General*, among other writings. The real in such case is, of course, a representation, a spectral projection that constitutes the amphibology of real-thought whereby it seems to be expected that a superior form of reality is to be *uncovered*—an *aletheia* to be brought forth—the truth. Therefore, the real becomes subject to gradation in worth; it is subjected to the process of valorisation or it is the product of value creation—it is less or more real depending on the truth-value assigned to it.

Revisiting Marx's claim that philosophy is the thought of the Universal Egoist by being centered on the subject, I would like to restate, concurring with both Marx and Laruelle, that indeed the incapacity to think from "a third person's perspective" is at the core of the principle of philosophical sufficiency (as discussed in the previous chapters). Without such tectonic epistemic shift, decentering the human is an always already failed act. In order to evade inflation of the human via post-humanism that inadvertently becomes transhumanism, I suggest to adopt an under-determination of "the human" or its philosophically impoverished conceptualisation. As Ó Maoilearca demonstrates, radical decentering is possible through abandoning the philosophical sufficiency of the human and assuming the perspective of a prelingual self. I have argued previously, in my interpretation of Marx, that the "prelingual self"—one that does not purport to be fully developed and self-sufficient subjectivity—can liken itself with "third objects" or see itself as an object. The non-human that inhabits such position is an animal or rather a non-animal or non-philosophically conceived animal (Ó Maoilearca, 2014: 115). When acceding to the plane of the transcendental by assuming the stance of radical subjectivity or of the stranger (Laruelle, 1995), the non-philosophical human enters the world (of philosophy) as an idiot in the ancient Greek sense of *idiotēs* but also in the Russian sense of *yurodivy* as taken up from Orthodox Christian mysticism and developed in Dostoevsky's *The Idiot* (and other novels). He or she is underdetermined by the knowledge of the world (as philosophy) while accessing it in her or his vulnerability or potentiality as a victim (Laruelle, 2012: 30).[1] Or as Ó Maoilearca puts it:

> He, or she, or it, then, is certainly not the "wise one," the master, but the Idiot—or, we might add, the stupid beast (bête bêtise). This turn to a "transcendental Idiot of an ante-decisional simplicity." (John O Maiolearca, 2014: 120)

---

[1] "Elle [la victime] se défini par une passivité radicale et non pas absolu comme celle que Levinas attribue au moi. La passivité radicale est celle qui par définition ne peut ré-agir par un excès de puissance ou surpuissance, il lui est impossible de ré-agir de manière réflexe, mais elle est capable d'agir tout autrement, par dépotentialisation de la surpuissance philosophique." (F. Laruelle, *Théorie générale des victimes*, Paris: Fayard 2012, p. 30.)

By way of "depotentialising" the human or man or ridding him of "philosophical overpotentialisation" (Laruelle, 2012: 30), the non-standard philosophy undertakes a procedure of radical decentering of thought determined by humanism's morphology clothing the supposed abstract notion of the subject as *anthropos*. Subjectivisation or projecting a subject onto the object of study retains the principle of philosophical sufficiency and its self-circumscription. Marx invites us—the humans, or us the idiots—to conceive of ourselves as objects. Philosophy is "philo-fiction" as Laruelle puts it (2010a) and it therefore permits the other possibility too: instead of subjectivising the universe, let us fictionalise the objectivisation of the self. Such would be the stance of science too as it submits to—and seeks to produce the Maßstab of—the real rather than the other way around.

The human may be a central category in Laruelle, something that Ray Brassier finds problematic (2005: 77–80), yet again it is neither anthropocentric nor a form of humanism. We have attempted to demonstrate in the previous chapters that humanism is essentially philosophical—it is founded upon the gesture of amphibology (of the real and thought, as per Laruelle), which inevitably produces ontologisation of human centrality. In Laruelle, however, humanity is an identity in the last instance, one among many, coupled with a determination in the last instance of the category of the real, a concept minimally philosophical and fundamentally materialist (therefore, historical too). It can be determined by the real of its fundamental vulnerability or "the persecution that renders it victim" (Laruelle, 2015) or otherwise, but the assumed plurality (of "otherwise") materialises itself "each time once" (Grelet, 2004) as the real is synonymous with the one. Thus it is one of the multitudes of realities but it is central to non-philosophy due to the fact that *philosophy is the product of human practice*—it is contingent on social relations and is determined in the last instance by the real of the species being of humanity. In short, it is central because it is a contingency, not an Absolute.

Haraway's proposal to treat the animals as "fellow laborers" (and why that is problematic)

Marx treats the displacement of the axis of thought from subjectivity centered to object centered as the prerequisite for establishing a science of "the species being of humanity." Let us revisit the following quote from Marx in order to compare it to a "Marxist feminist proposal" made by Haraway we will discuss immediately afterward.

> For this third object I am thus a *different reality* than itself; that is, I am *its* object. Thus, to suppose a being which is not the object of another being is to presuppose that *no* objective being exists. As soon as I have an object, this object has me for an object. But a *non-objective* being is an unreal, non-sensuous thing—a product of mere thought (i.e., of mere imagination)—an abstraction. To be *sensuous*, that is, to be really existing, means to be an object of sense, to be a *sensuous* object, to have sensuous objects outside oneself—objects of one's sensuousness. To be sensuous is to *suffer*. (Marx, *Economic-Philosophical Manuscripts of 1844*: "Critique of Hegel's Philosophy in General")

Haraway argues in a declaredly Marxian vein that "instrumentality" and a certain physical interconnectedness with other bodies that are defining of animals, but also of women, are inalienable from the human seen in its aspect of an animal, one among the other animal species.

> Best of all, the Marxist feminist in my history and community reminds me that freedom cannot be defined as the opposite of necessity if the mindful body in all its thickness is not to be disavowed, with all the vile consequences of such disavowal for those assigned to bodily entrammelment, such as women, the colonized, and the whole list of "others" who cannot live inside the illusion that freedom comes only when work and necessity are

shuffled off onto someone else. Instrumental relations have to be revalued, rethought, lived another way. (Haraway, 2007: 73)

In other words, by being instrumental to others we align ourselves with the needs of those others or simply we align and establish material continuity with others; we seek to clone or mimic them (not merely the needs but the others too in order to clone or grasp the needs), to act as their prosthesis in order to meet them and their needs. What we as Marxists ought to avoid in instrumentalisation is calculation, calculativeness, or calculative reason, insists Haraway (2007: 75, 78) following Derrida (2002). Haraway admits that scientific reason needs to operate with calculation but nonetheless purports that calculation has no place where the "multispecies responsibility is at stake" (Haraway, 2007: 81). I fail to understand why calculative reason in this respect is of defining importance and how Haraway's notion of "gradual freedom" (2007: 73) is not calculative in some sense. We are animals that sometimes need to kill animals, she admits, but a feminist Marxist dedicated to "multispecies responsibility" will not do it through "preset taxonomic calculation" (Haraway, 2007: 71). Instead, she argues that "human beings must learn to kill responsibly. And to be killed responsibly, yearning for the capacity to respond and to recognise response, always with reasons but knowing there will never be sufficient reason" (Haraway, 2007: 81). We must accept our sin and repent knowing the crime will never be redeemed. But, at least, we have killed "responsibly." This is not a Marxist feminist solution to the problem, but one of a Christian moralist.

The needed morality, in my view, is culturing a radical ability to remember and feel what is going on and performing the epistemological, emotional, and technical work to respond practically. (Haraway, 2007: 75)

Speaking as a Marxist, I would insist that it is not about the individual, it is not about the human subjectivity at the center of all killing, unprecedented until 200 years ago as Derrida puts it (2002: 417), but rather about centering the discussion on the political-economic conditions of capitalism and the "perspective" of those who are being killed on mass industrial scale.

In order to equate the human and the non-human animal in the chain of destruction that sustains economy and technology, or to render them equal in the instance of necessary killing, Haraway chooses to treat both the animal (including the lab animal and animals for slaughter) and the human animal as "laborers." But neither are "laborers" under the terms of capitalism. The system of capitalist economy does not recognise any other form of labor except "wage labor." The estranged, abstracted wage labor, the abstraction of labor turned into a self-standing reality and commodity (in the narrower economic sense) as reified abstraction are the creation of philosophy and, by structural homology, of capitalism too. By the same token, the wage laborer is by definition human and, in his determination in the last instance, a male human, also more often than not—white. Wage labor is applicable to humans only, or to be more concise—to man only. Women and animals are resource, material, as will become men too with the extinction of the wage laborer—the flesh necessary for the combustion of the Machine-Capital. Haraway seeks to "emancipate" the animal through this move, and in spite of her declared expansion of the category of the animal to include the human, a gesture of subjectivisation of the killed or the suffering animal takes place. Therefore, in spite of the opposite intention, animal's humanisation takes place. She is elevating both the human and the non-human animal into laborers, which implies both agency and "meaningful purpose" of existence (or productiveness)—her solution is too "philosomorphic" (to borrow the term from Ó Maoilearca).

Indeed, some creatures, such as animals and women and some people of color, cannot estrange their labor from their "true selves" and, therefore, see liberation in the time off from the machine of wage labor. The liberation conceived in such a way relies on a presupposition about the universal validity of the body/mind divide, which can be projected upon oneself more successfully by men than by women, and then more successfully by humans than by animals. Along the lines of such projection, the wage laborer and capitalism-as-philosophy can assume that, although the body and labor in its mechanicity are temporarily "rented" for wage, the true self, the Cogito remains presumably free. It is thereon presumed that the freedom of the "true self" (the Cogito) is effectuated in the time away from the workplace or in leisure. However, animals and women cannot establish a sharp separation between their presumed "true self" (or the Cogito) and the body—such divide is essentially masculine argue both Haraway (2007: 77–79) and Derrida (2002: 407–418).

> (Derrida understood that patricide and fratricide are the only real murders in the logic of humanism; everybody else to whom the law is applied is covered by courtesy.) The substitute, the scapegoat, is not Man but Animal. (Haraway, 2007: 79)

Therefore, the idea of emancipation or liberation through improvement of wage laborers' rights (and the right to not work either for wage or simply not to work *tout court*) is also essentially masculine. Women and animals establish corporal continuity with other creatures and it is a continuity that can also be instrumental. Therefore, women and animals are by necessity but also willingly instrumental to others. The necessity in question is not always the result of external constriction but quite often willed as in maternity. When, on the other hand, it is a matter of constriction and recognised as necessity, the liberation is found in the affinity with others albeit subjected to instrumentalisation that can involve pain and even killing, argues Haraway (2007: 74, 77–82). Haraway's feminist reading of the idea of emancipation as "free time" from waged work as essentially masculine and, therefore, deficient is something I would subscribe to. I would also subscribe to the idea that one can and should seek liberation precisely in and through the practice of acting as an extension (prosthesis and "companionship") to other beings, as both mental and corporal. However, the industrialisation of such processes and their preconditioning as capitalist reduces the animal and the woman to commodities or "passive matter" (or the use value of commodities) rather than elevate them to the status of "laborers." They are not active agents or subjects endowed with intentionality of companionship or production. A lab animal is no wage laborer: it does not receive wage and is unable to alienate its labor in order to become a wage laborer. Laborers other than wage laborers do not exist in capitalism. Labor that has not been recognised as such through monetary valorisation—does not receive wage and does not enter nation-states' calculations counting money, e.g., GDB—is no labor to capitalism. It is material; it is capital investment (lab animals) or social reproduction (women). It has only use value and is reduced to the practice of use. Thus no subjectivisation into "laborers" is possible. Moreover, it is not strategically desirable (even if hypothetically possible) as it does not serve the socialist argument but merely thwarts the analysis in order to render the capitalist holocaust of animals bearable. They are commodities that serve the use value of combustion of their materiality. Their holocaust is the origin of the aerial reality of not only surplus value but of value *tout court* or of the Absolute. Haraway was more precise when she wrote:

> Simian orientalism means that western primatology has been about the construction of the self from the raw material of the other, the appropriation of nature in the production of culture, the ripening of the human from the soil of the animal, the clarity of white from the obscurity of color, the issue of man from the body of woman, the elaboration of gender from the resource of sex, the emergence of mind by the activation of body. To effect these transformative operations, simian "orientalist" discourse must first construct the terms: animal, nature, body, primitive, female. (Haraway, 1989: 11)

Similarly to Haraway, Laruelle proposes a set of species shared by human and non-human animals as means of democratisation of political-economic thought and practice, but this set is without human morphology. The likening between the two categories takes place through the shared determination in the last instance; they are both—or rather all—"victims-in-person" (Laruelle, 2012: 148–149). They are not abstractions reified as general entities or entities (as if) general, i.e., endlessly expanded particularities whose determination in the last instance is not shared by the entities it seeks to encompass. The generalisation consists in the procedure of thought (without pretension for ontologisation) yielding into the constitution of a category of victim-in-person that operates as a set that comprises all those in person that could fall under the same category or be included in the set. (The use of the concept of set is mine whereas Laruelle resorts to tropes from quantum theory and the procedure of superposition, which is, however, relevant for the human perspective and human ability for identification. I am concerned, however, with the possibility of constitution of a single category without resorting to human psychology including the ability of identification.) When it comes to enabling animals to "escape from the vicious circle of massacre," in Laruelle's analysis (2012: 148–149), it remains a human political question and practical task—the animals do not need to be subjected to ontological reconceptualisation. They should not be expected to enact a new and different ontology in order to "escape the vicious circle." The animals do not need to become a different reality in order to fit the proposed new ontology that will enable their liberation. They need to be released from the (philosophical) encirclement at issue by assigning them different "use in the last instance" (Laruelle, 2012: 149). Unlike Haraway, Laruelle does not propose a "revalorisation" of animal life or resignification that stamps on the animal different value (one that signals it should not be "killable," as Haraway would put it). Laruelle does not propose revaluing of values. He proposes assigning different *use*, taken away from use value as an aspect of exchange value and reduced to its sheer materiality preceding signification.

The "General Animal"

By anthropomorphising animal use in capitalist production by way of declaring it "labor"—lab and farm animals are to be seen as "unpaid workers" doing their work for the love of work instead of wage?—and proposing the concept of "Companion Species," Haraway executes an act of philosophical decisionism. She institutes an amphibology of thought and the real by introducing an abstraction into the realm of the real or as the real, similarly to the grotesque idea of the "General Animal" Marx writes about in the first edition of the first volume of *Capital*. Before we discuss that passage by Marx, let us consider Derrida, the author on whose considerations Haraway bases her proposals of "responsible killing" and the creation of "companion species" as aspects of animal workforce.

> The confusion of all nonhuman living creatures within the general and common category of the animal is not simply a sin against rigorous thinking, vigilance, lucidity, or empirical authority; it is also a crime. Not against animality precisely, but a crime of the first order against the animals, against animals. (Derrida, 2002: 417)

They are commodity or mere use value precisely because they are reduced to "the animal in general" or to "the Animal." They are the abstraction that supplants the real animals whereas the latter are its reifications in the sense of resource or material for commodity production. Marx uses the example of the general category of the animal in order to explain the absurdity of the reified general equivalent or commodity as monetary entity according to its determination in the last instance.

> It is as if alongside and external to lions, tigers, rabbits, and all other actual animals, which form when grouped together the various kinds, species, subspecies, families etc. of the animal kingdom, there existed also in addition

the animal, the individual incarnation of the entire animal kingdom. (Marx, *Capital*, Vol. I, Chapter 1 of the first edition)[2]

As previously explained, to treat the general equivalent as the real or as if real in the sense of physical entity and the other way around, namely to reduce the real animals to the general animal (not as real abstraction in Sohn-Rethel's sense but as "incarnation of the entire animal kingdom"), is to reify an abstraction. It constitutes the founding gesture of capitalism. A similar gesture grounds and sustains patriarchy and heteronormative sexuality—the general equivalent of woman or the woman as reified abstraction. "What does a Woman want?," asks the male philosopher. The question is incomprehensible to an everyday, real, and concrete woman or to the real (non-abstract) women. It is, however, comprehensible to male philosophers and they are able to converse on the topic and create a supposedly universally legible discourse (in the universe of patriarchal reason). Nonetheless, neither woman nor the animal is serious topic enough for a proper philosophical discussion. They are, however, adequate for philosophical anecdotal use. Man, capitalist value, and philosophy are born from the founding sacrificial gesture of slaughter and *holokaustos* of the general animal. They are sustained, however, by the general slaughter of real animals. The logic of it all is amphibologic—the metaphysics of supplanting the real with the thought that purports to be the perfected real, i.e., "the philosophical truth" or the being (of something or in general). The founding gesture of all philosophy, as defined by Laruelle, seems to provide the support for the political economy of capitalism and for a patriarchy in which women and everyone else exist (or are not killed by virtue of law) only "by courtesy" (Haraway, 2007: 79). Derrida writes of the destruction of animals and the constitution of the animal (and, therefore, the man) in a similar

---

[2]The first edition in English translation is available in Albert Dragstedt, *Value: Studies by Karl Marx*, London: New Park Publications, 1976, pp. 7–40.

fashion or in line with the diagnostics of philosophy in general proffered by Laruelle (and indirectly by Marx):

> The gesture seems to me to constitute philosophy as such, the philosopheme itself. (2002: 408)

By the same token, women and animals are excluded from philosophy and from the realm of agencies of capitalist production too. Let us reiterate, they are not laborers as labor that counts; labor that is recognised and compensated for is only wage labor. The one who can effectively estrange his labor, the one who can split his time between work hours and leisure, the one who can effectively enact the body/mind divide is the man. As Haraway rightly notices in her close reading of Derrida, we, women and animals, are not killed by courtesy only (2007: 79).

Along the same lines, we can infer that gay men, men of color, men of religion that does not belong to the "Greek-Judean" tradition undergirded by European philosophy are too included in humanity by courtesy only. That is why subjection, exploitation, and brutality toward some categories of human beings require "de-humanisation" or reduction to an animal. By adopting a complete reversal of the humanist reason and its sometimes unintended procedures of dehumanisation, we can conclude that it is only by the emancipation of the animal that the marginalised and exploited parts of humanity can be freed from suffering and killing.

Post-humanism can accomplish its goal of human decentering only by way of emancipating the non-human, beginning with the animal. Animal seen as "mere machine" can be destroyed with no regard of inflicted pain—the screams of pain are mere illusion; they are not true because philosophy has decided animals are mere machines free of feelings and bereft of self-consciousness. They do not possess a self as they do not possess reason. Thus, animals are further reduced to machines, or the animal is further reduced to machine, so that dehumanisation is complete and the holocaust can be flawlessly accomplished. In conclusion, the animal and the machine do not occupy opposite positions. Quite the contrary, they are similarly devalued or exposed in their absence of value—they are devoid of sense; they are numb physicality insofar as they are the real that precedes language. They are mindless. Since Descartes, the animals have been explained as machines or have been seen as animated machines:

> Now a very large number of the motions occurring inside us do not depend in any way on the mind. These include heartbeat, digestion, nutrition, respiration when we are asleep, and also such waking actions as walking, singing, and the like, when these occur without the mind attending to them. When people take a fall, and stick out their hands so as to protect their head, it is not reason that instructs them to do this; it is simply that the sight of the impending fall reaches the brain and sends the animal spirits into the nerves in the manner necessary to produce this movement even without any mental volition, just as it would be produced in a machine. (1989: 229–230)

In Descartes, life is equated with reason and with the absence of any physicality, with the cancellation of the possibility of any movement pertaining to physicality. To claim that life is sublimated in its perfection called mind or reason is to say that mind or reason is pure and perfect life, the substance of life independent from materiality, pure volition as pure reason. I do not see why such thesis would be less vitalist than the one that argues that life transpires though physical world too. The contempt for the physical world in Descartes is all-encompassing; both animals (including the human body) and machines are *automata* or lifeless moving structures. Life is valued as pure life or as pure value of life. What is devalued and transformed into an object of exploitation is matter itself. It is also an object of destruction for the sake of pleasure.

The experience of pleasure derives from the obsessive-compulsive urge to erase all traces of life as messy flesh and mindless machine. Constant cleaning, erasure, reduction of the automaton of the body to the machinic automaton is the move of philosophical amphibology that institutes the real by way of amphibology. In order to erase the last remaining trace of messy materiality acting as the reminder of the fact that the real is indifferent to thought, meaning, or truth, one must transform the automaton into a machine of making sense. Hence, by an act of ultimate Hegelian sublation, the phantasm of the omnipotent AGI is created—the senseless automaton has been transformed into an automaton of pure sense. "Rationalism," based on its opposition to "emotionalism" (Power, 2016), is enabled by another opposition whose identity in the last instance is the dualism of Western religion and its other, namely secularism whose philosophical reconciliation or dialectical synthesis is—(Western) civilisation—materially determined by the *massacres of the less human* (Anidjar, 2006: 52–77).

> Christianity slowly granted other communities and traditions—those it exploited or converted, massacred and "civilized," enslaved and exterminated—new structures of authority and domination, new and newly negotiable configurations of power. (Anidjar, 2006: 60)

Emotions are too reminiscent of physicality as they invoke screams of pain and shrieks of pleasure. They are removed from the automaton of making sense—the supplanting of the real with sense aims at installing truth as the real, as more perfect real than the real itself. That is the gesture that grounds all philosophy. The act of amphibology is enacted—the real is decided by philosophy and truth is put in the stead of the real as a higher form of real. The fetishes of reason and value are inherently conditioned by the destruction of the material universe. Marx was right; the emancipation of materiality insofar as physicality, living or non-living, is also the way out of philosophy and toward the establishment of a science of the species being of humanity. Laruelle would say it is the only way toward establishing "science of the humans [in plural]," provided humanity is treated in its identity in the last instance as one among the many phenomena in the vast out-there without assigning it any special status. In doing so, we have to start by coming to terms with what we did to the animals in the constitutive act of philosophy and via proxy to all those dehumanised that belong to the species of man "by courtesy" only.

LIST OF REFERENCES

Abelson, Harold et Gerald Jay Sussman (1996) *Structure and Interpretation of Computer Programs*. Cambridge, MA: MIT Press.

Agamben, Giorgio (2005) *State of Exception*. Trans. Kevin Attell. Chicago: University of Chicago Press.

Alexiou, Margaret (2002) *The Ritual Lament in Greek Tradition*. 2nd ed. Revised by Dimitrios Yatromanolakis and Panagiotis Roilos. Lanham, MD: Rowman & Littlefield Publishers.

Anidjar, Gil (2014) *Blood: A Critique of Christianity*. New York: Columbia University Press.

Anidjar, Gil (2006) "Secularism." *Critical Inquiry* 33, no. 1: 52–77.

Benjamin, Walter (1999) *Selected Writings*. Vols. I–II. Cambridge, MA: Harvard UP/Belknap.

Braidotti, Rosi (2013) *The Posthuman*. Cambridge, UK: Polity Press.

Brassier, Ray (2005) "Liquider l'homme une fois pour toutes." In Gilles Grelet (ed.) *Théorie-rébellion: Un ultimatum*. Paris: l'Harmattan.

Brassier, Ray (2009) "Liquidate Man Once and for All." Written in 2005 published on the *In/Appearance* blog. Available at https://inappearance.wordpress.com/2009/11/03/liquidate-man-once-and-for-all/, accessed on April 28, 2018.

Butler, Judith (2006) *Precarious Life: The Power of Mourning and Violence*. London and New York: Verso Books.

Butler, Judith (2004) *Undoing Gender*. London and New York: Routledge.

Chomsky, Noam (1959) "On Certain Formal Properties of Grammars." *Information and Control* 2, no. 2: 137–167.

Cockshott, Paul (2012) "Turing: The Irruption of Materialism into Thought." *Oxford University Press's Blog: Academic Insights for the Thinking World*. Available at https://blog.oup.com/2012/06/turing-the-irruption-of-materialism-into-thought/, accessed on April 15, 2018.

Cockshott, Paul, Lewis M. Mackenzie and Greg Michaelson (2015) *Computation and Its Limits*. Oxford, UK: Oxford University Press.

Cuboniks, Laboria (2015) *Xenofeminism: A Politics of Alienation*. Available at http://www.laboriacuboniks.net/#firstPage, accessed on July 16, 2018.

DeLanda, Manuel (2002) *Intensive Science and Virtual Philosophy*. London and New York: Continuum.

Deleuze, Gilles and Felix Guattari (1987) *A Thousand Plateaus: Capitalism and Schizophrenia*. Trans. Brian Massumi. Minneapolis: University of Minnesota Press.

Dennett, Daniel (2017) *From Bacteria to Bach and Back: The Evolution of Minds*. New York: W. W. Norton & Company.

Derrida, Jacques (1998) *Of Grammatology*. Trans. Gayatri Chakravorty Spivak. Baltimore, MD: Johns Hopkins University Press.

Derrida, Jacques (2002) "The Animal That Therefore I Am (More to Follow)." Trans. David Wills, *Critical Inquiry* 28: 369–418.

Descartes, René (1989) *Passions of the Soul*. Trans. Stephen H. Voss. Indianapolis: Hackett.

Foucault, Michel (1966) *Les Mots et les choses*. Paris: Éditions Gallimard.

Gangle, Rocco and Julius Greve (2017) *Superpositions Volume: Laruelle and the Humanities*. Lanham, MD: Rowman & Littlefield.

Grelet, Gilles (2004) "Anti-phénoménologie." *Revue philosophique de la France et de l'étranger: Presses Universitaires de France* 129-Tom 2: 211–224.

Gruntman, Michal, Dorothee Groß, Maria Májeková and Katja Tielbörger (2017) "Decision-Making in Plants under Competition." *Nature Communications* 8, no. 2235.

Haraway, Donna (1985) "Manifesto for Cyborgs: Science, Technology, and Socialist Feminism in the 1980's." *Socialist Review* 80: 65–108.

Haraway, Donna (1989) *Primate Visions: Gender, Race and Nature in the World of Modern Science*. New York and London: Routledge.

Haraway, Donna (1991) "A Cyborg Manifesto: Science, Technology, and Socialist-Feminism in the Late Twentieth Century." In *Simians, Cyborgs and Women: The Reinvention of Nature*. London and New York: Routledge, 149–181.

Haraway, Donna (1995) "Cyborgs and Symbionts: Living Together in the New World Order." In Chris Hables-Gray (ed.) *The Cyborg Handbook*. London and New York: Routledge.

Haraway, Donna (2007) *When Species Meet*. (Posthumanities). Minneapolis: University of Minnesota Press.

Haraway, Donna (2015) "Anthropocene, Capitalocene, Plantationocene, Chthulucene: Making Kin." *Environmental Humanities* 6: 159–165.

Haraway, Donna (2016) "Tentacular Thinking: Anthropocene, Capitalocene, and Chtulucene." *E-Flux* 75, http://www.e-flux.com/journal/75/67125/tentacular-thinking-anthropocene-capitalocene-chthulucene/, accessed on June 2017.

Hayles, Katherine (1999) *How We Became Posthuman: Virtual Bodies in Cybernetics, Literature, and Informatics*. Chicago: University of Chicago Press.

Henry, Michel (1983) *Marx: A Philosophy of Human Reality*. Trans. Kathleen McLaughlin and Michel Henry. Bloomington, IN: Indiana University Press.

Irigaray, Luce (1985a) *This Sex Which Is Not One*. Trans. Catherine Porter and Carolyn Burke. Ithaca, NY: Cornell University Press.

Irigaray, Luce (1985b) *Speculum of the Other Woman*. Trans. Gillian C. Gill. Ithaca, NY: Cornell University Press.

Kolozova, Katerina, and Zarko Trajanoski, eds. (2001) *Conversations with Judith Butler*. Skopje: Euro-Balkan Press.

Kolozova, Katerina (2015) *Toward Radical Metaphysics of Socialism: Marx and Laruelle*. New York Brooklyn: Punctum Books.

Lacan, J. (1998) *The Seminar of Jacques Lacan, Book XI: The Four Fundamental Concepts of Psychoanalysis*. Ed. Jacques-Alain Miller. Trans. Alan Sheridan. New York/London: W. W. Norton and Company.

Laruelle, François (1978) "Pour une linguistique active (la notion de phonèse)." *Revue philosophique de la France et de l'étranger* 168, no. 4 (October–December 1978): 419–431.

Laruelle, François (1989) *Philosophie et non-philosophie*. Liège – Bruxelles: Pierre Mardaga.

Laruelle, François (1992) *Théorie des identités*. Paris: Presses Universitaires de France.

Laruelle, François (1995) *Théorie des Étrangers: Science des hommes, démocratie et non-psychanalyse*. Paris: Éditions Kimé.

Laruelle, François (2010a) *Philosophie Non-Standard: Générique, Quantique, Philo-Fiction*. Paris: Kimé.

Laruelle, François (2010b) *Philosophies of Difference: A Critical Introduction to Non-philosophy*. Trans. Rocco Gangle. London: Bloomsbury.

Laruelle, François (2012) *Théorie générale des victims*. Paris: Fayard.

Laruelle, François (2013a) *Philosophy and Non-Philosophy*. Trans. Taylor Adkins. Minneapolis: University of Minnesota Press—Univocal Publishing.

Laruelle, François (2013b) "The Transcendental Computer." A chapter from the Collection *Homo Ex Machina* (l'Harmattan, 2005). Translated from the French by Taylor Adkins and Chris Eby, *Speculative Heresy*. Available at https://speculativeheresy.wordpress.com/2013/08/26/translation-of-f-laruelles-the-transcendental-computer-a-non-philosophical-utopia/, accessed on January 18, 2018.

Laruelle, François (2014) *Introduction to Non-Marxism*. Trans. Anthony Paul Smith. Minneapolis: University of Minnesota Press-Univocal Publishing.

Laruelle, François (2015) *General Theory of Victims*. Trans. Jessie Hock and Alex Dubilet. Hoboken, NJ: Wiley.

Laruelle, François (2016) *Theory of Identities*. Trans. Alyosha Edlebi. New York: Columbia University Press.

Levi-Strauss, Claude (1969) *The Elementary Structures of Kinship*. Trans. James Bell Harle under the supervision of Rodney Needham. Boston: Beacon Press.

Löffler, Davor (2017) *Rekursion zivilisatorischer Kapazitäten als Entwicklungsmuster in der Zivilisationsgeschichte*. Doctoral Dissertation defended at Freie Universität in Berlin.

Löffler, Davor (2018) "Distributing Potentiality. Post-Capitalist Economies and the Generative Time Regime Distributing Potentiality." *Identities: Journal for Politics, Gender and Culture* 15, no. 1–2: 8–45.

Marx, Karl (1956) *Capital: Volume II*. Trans. I. Lasker. Moscow: Progress Publishers. Available at https://www.marxists.org/archive/marx/works/1885-c2/.

Marx, Karl (1959) *Economic and Philosophical Manuscripts of 1844*. Moscow: Progress Publishers. Available at https://www.marxists.org/archive/marx/works/download/pdf/Economic-Philosophic-Manuscripts-1844.pdf, accessed on July 1, 2018.

Marx, Karl and F. Engels (1967) *Werke, Ergänzungsband, 1. Teil*. Berlin: Dietz Verlag.

Marx, Karl (1968) *A Critique of the German Ideology*. Moscow: Progress Publishers.

Marx, Karl (1969a) *Theses on Feuerbach*. Translated from the German by W. Lough. Moscow USSR: Progress Publishers. Available at https://www.marxists.org/archive/marx/works/1845/theses/theses.htm, accessed on March 22, 2019.

Marx, Karl and Frederick Engels (1969b) "Manifesto of the Communist Party." In Karl Marx and Frederick Engels (eds.) *Selected Works, Vol. 1: 1845–1859*. Moscow: Progress Publishers.

Marx, Karl (1973) *Grundrisse: Outlines of the Critique of Political Economy*. Trans. Martin Nicolaus. New York: Penguin Books, 1973.

Marx, Karl (1978) *Capital: Volume I*. Trans. Samuel Moore and Edward Aveling. Ed. Frederick Engels. Moscow: Progress Publishers. Available at https://www.marxists.org/archive/marx/works/1867-c1/.

Marx, Karl (1996; 1999) *Capital*. Vol. III. Ed. Frederick Engels, from the online version of the Marxist Internet Archive (1996; 1999). Available at www.marxists.org/archive/marx/works/1894-c3, accessed on May 5, 2018.

Moulinier, Louis (1950) Le pur et l'impur dans la pensée et la sensibilité des Grecs jusqu' à la fin du IVeme siècle av. J.C: Thèse à la Faculté des lettres de l'Université de Paris.

Ó Maoilearca, J. (2014) "The Animal Line: On the Possibility of a 'Laruellean' Non-Human Philosophy." *Angelaki: Journal of the Theoretical Humanities* 19, no. 2: 113–129.

Ó Maoilearca, J. (2015) *All Thoughts Are Equal: Laruelle and Nonhuman Philosophy*. (Posthumanities). Minneapolis: University of Minnesota Press.

Power, Nina (2016) "Philosophy, Sexism, Emotion, Rationalism." In Eileen Joy and Katerina Kolozova (eds.) *After the "Speculative Turn": Realism, Philosophy and Feminism*. Brooklyn, NY: Punctum Books.

Roden, David (2014) *Posthuman Life: Philosophy at the Edge of the Human*. London: Routledge.

Saussure, Ferdinand de (1959) *Course in General Linguistics*. Ed. Charles Bally and Albert Reidlinger. Trans. Wade Baskin. New York: Philosophical Library.

Schmid, Anne-Françoise (2015) "On Contemporary Objects." In Robin Mackay (ed.) *Simulation, Exercise, Operations*. Falmouth, UK: Urbanomic Press.

Schmitt, Carl. 1985. *Political Theology*. Trans. Georg D. Schwab. Cambridge, MA: MIT Press.

Sellars, W. (1963) *Science, Perception and Reality*. London: Routledge and Kegan Paul.

Simondon, Gilbert (2007) *L'Individuation Psychique et Collective: à la lumière de Forme, Information, Potentiel et Métastabilité*. Paris: Aubier.

Smith, Anthony Paul (2013) *A Non-Philosophical Theory of Nature: Ecologies of Thought*. New York: Palgrave Macmillan.

Sohn-Rethel, Alfred (1978) *Intellectual and Manual Labor: Critique of Epistemology*. London: Macmillan.

Spinoza, Benedict de. (2003) *The Ethics*. Trans. R. H. M. Elwes. The Project Gutenberg Etext Publication. Available at http://www.gutenberg.org/etext/3800.

Turing, Alan (1950) "Computing Machinery and Intelligence." *Mind* 49: 433–460.

Turing, Alan (1986) "Proposal for Development in the Mathematics Division of an Automatic Computing Engine (ACE)." *A.M. Turing's ACE Report of 1946 and Other Papers*. Ed. B. E. Carpenter and R. W. Doran. Cambridge, MA: MIT Press.

Vernant, Jean-Pierre (1983) *Myth and Thought among the Greeks*. Trans. Janet Lloyd and Jeff Fort. Cambridge, MA: MIT Press and Zone Books.

Vernant, Jean-Pierre (1984) *The Origins of Greek Thought*. Ithaca, NY: Cornell University Press.

Vernant, Jean-Pierre (1995) *La mort dans les yeux. Figures de l'Autre en Grèce ancienne: Artémis, Gorgô*. Paris: HachetteVerso Books.

Williams, Donald Cary (1953) "On the Direct Probability of Inductions." *Mind* 62: 465–483.
Wittgenstein, Ludwig (1922) *Tractatus Logico-Philosophicus*. London: Kegan Paul, Trench, Trubner & Co., Ltd. Available at Gutenberg project, accessed on November 2017.
Wolfe, Cary (2009) *What Is Posthumanism?* Minneapolis: University of Minnesota Press.
Wolfe, Cary (2013) *Before the Law: Animals in a Biopolitical Context*. Chicago, IL: University of Chicago Press.
Wood, Allen (2005) "Karl Marx." In Honderich, Ted (ed.) *The Oxford Companion to Philosophy*. Oxford: Oxford University Press, 212–213.
Wynter, Sylvia (1982) "Beyond Liberal and Marxist Leninist Feminisms: Towards an Autonomous Frame of Reference," a paper presented at the Annual Conference of the American Sociological Association held in San Francisco.

INDEX

Abelson, Harold 58, 63
abstraction
    fetishised 37, 111
    pure 92, 105, 128
    real 10, 35, 51, 56–8, 61, 69, 71, 73, 79–80, 84, 128, 147
    reified 30, 37, 126, 142, 147
    self-standing 90, 92–3, 131
ACE (Automatic Computing Engine) 62
Adkins, Taylor 6 n.1
    blog "Speculative Heresy" 33
Agamben, Giorgio 110
Alexiou, Margaret 110
alienation 66, 84, 123–31
amphibology 16–17, 38, 98, 136–7, 139, 146, 150
Anidjar, Gil 136, 150
    massacres of the less human 150
animal-for-killing 27–8, 135, 137, 139, 141, 143, 145, 147, 149
    abolishment, possibilities 135–9
animality 1–12, 18–20, 23, 28, 37, 45–6, 70–1, 79, 115, 121–2, 146
    in capitalist machine 18–20
    femaleness 2, 24
    in hybridity with the automation of signification 12, 24, 27, 57–9
animal-machine 11, 27, 148–50
    capitalist automaton 91–2
    origin and power 58–60
animals. *See also* holocaust
    exploitation 23, 54, 148–9
    as fellow laborers 140–5 (*See also* Haraway, Donna)
    General Animal, idea of 146–51 (*See also* Marx, Karl)
    killing or suffering 27–8, 135–9
    as mere machines 148–9

prosthesis (or technology) 4, 103, 129, 141, 144
    rights 52
    self 129
    use value 54
    and women 142–3, 148
anthropocentrism 1, 3, 8–9, 12, 19, 25, 43, 69, 82, 133, 139. *See also* Foucalt, Michel
anthropomorphism 101–2, 127, 135, 146
Aristotle 21
artificial intelligence (AI) 65, 105
asymmetries 12, 26–7, 31–3, 102, 113, 128
atomism, Epicurean principle of *clinamen* 101
automated self 2, 106
automaton. *See also* transcendence
    of capital 26–7, 37, 107, 114–15, 117, 119–20, 123, 132
    of computer languages 41
    fetishisation 37, 46, 116
    full formalisation of categories 34–42
    fundamental concepts 30–1
    human animality or femaleness 2, 24
    hybridity 12
    language as 29–30
    of life 106
    market 56
    material process 106, 107
    M-C-M 17–18, 27, 113–18
    M-M 18, 113–18
    and patriarchy 26–7, 37, 113–15, 116, 119–20, 122, 132
    P(hallus)-F-P(hallus) 27, 113–18
    physicality of 11–13, 18–24, 26–35, 37, 39, 41–7, 49–53, 56–60, 68–72, 82–6, 90–2, 102–7, 116–20, 122–4, 149–50

INDEX

P-P 27, 120, 122
   of signification 12–13, 34, 48, 60, 70, 82, 114, 121, 123, 126, 130
   techno-capital 103
   transcendental inventions of humanity 107
   use value 36–7, 46, 48, 52, 54
autonomy 3, 59
auto-referentiality 13, 26
axiom 18–20, 50–1, 97, 104
   exploitation 51

being, the 13, 39
   before-the-other 74
   exteriority 74
   flesh 118
   human-in-human 70
   human too 53
   in-the-out-there 74
Benjamin, Walter 109–10
   "divine violence" 108
bestiality 120–2
binaries 31, 114, 131
biotechnologies 4
body
   exploitation 110
   female/woman 132–3, 144
   human production 93
   killable aspects 19, 23
   mind and 85, 91, 140, 143, 148
   physical 111, 120
   power of activity 51
   prelingual self 126–7
   spirit and 94
   transcendence 24, 44
Braidotti, Rosi 2–3, 3
Brassier, Ray 43, 43 n.2, 139
   "Liquidate Man Once and for All" 43
Brouzes, Etienne 79
Butler, Judith 52–3, 125
   Precarious Life: The Power of Mourning and Violence 52

capital 16–17, 19, 26–7, 37, 107, 114–15, 117, 119–20, 123, 132
   circulation of 17, 38, 119
   value exchange system 29
capitalism. *See also* value, exchange
   animal workforce 146–51
   anti- 23
   automata 27–8
   commodification of life 3
   exploitation of materials 20, 103, 108–10
   founding gesture 147
   logics 20
   military, technological development 2
   as-philosophy 28, 42
   physicality 16–17, 19, 21, 23–6, 28, 42, 45–7, 54, 93–5, 109–10, 130–1, 142, 144, 147
   post-2007 crisis 19
   subjectivity 98–105
Chomsky, Noam 30
chôra 6, 16, 21, 51, 61, 73, 97
circulation analysis 17–19, 38, 119
   Death-Life-Death abstraction 92
   rapid 18
   simple 17, 38, 119
clone 15, 23, 39, 60–2, 69, 73–8, 80, 82–4, 106–7, 141. *See also* thought, posture of
cloning 11, 25, 39, 61, 64, 73, 75–8, 106
Cockshott, Paul, *Computation and Its Limits* 63
codes/coding 26, 30, 64, 68, 74, 98, 106
commodification 16, 81, 110, 117
commodities 17–18, 27
communism 8, 81–2, 91, 95
computer languages 29–30, 41, 56–7, 68
computing 44, 56–8, 62–5, 68–9
consciousness 35–6, 47–8, 60, 62–5, 97
Cuboniks, Laboria 129, 131–2
   alienation, notion of 129

INDEX

culture 25, 31, 67–8, 110, 114–15, 121, 123, 132, 144
cyborgs 2–4, 12, 23, 27, 120–1, 123, 129. *See also* inhumanity

dehumanisation 46–7, 148, 151
DeLanda, Manuel 136
Deleuze, Gilles 57
dematerialisation 45, 117–18
Dennett, Daniel 43
Derrida, Jacques 27, 30, 141–3, 146–8
   on animal workforce 146–8
   on destruction of animals 147
Descartes, Rene 149
destruction 19–20, 27–8, 45, 48, 51, 54, 111, 142, 147, 149–50
determination in the last instance, of 6, 9, 17, 18, 21–2, 24, 35, 45, 51–2, 61–84. *See also* real; wage labor
   abolishment of animal for killing 139, 142, 145–6
   automata of capital and patriarchy 114–17, 126, 128
   identity, of/in the last instance 23, 34, 42, 44–5, 59–62
   identity, as fetish 37, 44, 115–16, 120, 124
   identity, as reification 37, 118
   materialist reason 61–2, 72, 78–9, 83–4, 86–7
   radical dyad 30, 35, 45, 50–1
   subjectivity 92, 103–4, 107–9
dialectics 2, 6–7, 13, 24, 31, 38, 67, 128, 130, *See also* metaphysics
   subject-object 26
Dostoevsky, Fyodor, *The Idiot* 138

egoism 92, 105, 128
emotions 51, 71, 132–3, 150
Engels, Frederick 8, 10, 94–5, 105 n.2, 118
   "Manifesto of the Communist Party" 7–8, 94, 118
exit philosophy 7–8, 10, 15–16, 25, 34, 42, 96, 100

explication 25, 34, 44, 55
exploitation 2, 20, 23
   female bodies 122–3
   of weak 132
exteriority 5–6, 13–15, 21

female/femaleness 24, 115–18, 133
   animal through fetishisation 119–23
   bodies, exploitation 122–3, 132
   human animality 2, 24
femininity 37, 78–9, 114–15, 117–18, 120–1, 132
feminism 13–17. *See also* cyborgs; Marxist feminism; xeno-feminism
   branches 121
   rationalism 133
   universalism and 25
fetishisation 16–17, 23, 35–7, 44, 72, 115–16, 119
finitude 6, 15
formalisation
   of categories 34–42
   of language 70–3
formalism
   automatism 68–9
   computerised signification 62–6
   creation of categories 74–81
   machines' agency 58–62 81–5
   materiality 25, 55–8
   non-Marxism 40
   non-philosophical treatment 67–8, 81–7
   radical concepts 81–7
Foucault, Michel 1–2
Freud, Sigmund 7

Gangle, Rocco 136
gender 38, 78–81, 120, 122, 132–3, 144
   abolitionism 133
   normative 120
   progressive 132
   roles 79–80
Grelet, Gilles 139
Greve, Julius 136

Gruntman, Michal 68
Guattari, Felix 57

Haraway, Donna 11–12, 12, 19, 23–4, 120–4, 128–9, 142–8. *See also* cyborgs
   inhuman, comparison 4
   "Man by courtesy only" 28
   "Manifesto for Cyborgs: Science, Technology, and Socialist Feminism in the 1980's" 2–4
   on "Marxist feminist proposal" 140–1
Hayles, Katherine 2
Hegel, Georg Wilhelm Friedrich 20–1
Henry, Michel 9–10, 84, 89–90, 95–6
holocaust 20, 23, 54, 110–11, 115, 120–1, 132, 144, 148
holokaustos (hiereia) 110–11, 117, 147
homologous 4, 10–11, 40, 67
human animal 28, 47, 58, 102, 135–6, 142
human-in-human 4–5
   exteriority 125–6
humanism 1–2, 8, 19. *See also* anthropocentrism post-humanism
   anti- 4, 12
   Marx's philosophy 89–90, 92, 95, 97, 102
   naturalism and 8, 48, 91, 131
   new definition 4
   philosophical 135–6
   trans 46, 138
humanity 7, 9, 12, 15–16, 18–20
   indispensable alienation 123–9
   "species being" 9, 15, 26, 28, 30, 38, 54–5, 59–60, 66, 79, 80–1, 83, 96, 100, 123–4, 127, 130, 139–40, 150
humans
   activity 9, 24
   animalism 2
   and humanism 4
   life and physical aspects 1–2
   philosophical projection (I or self) 124–5
   self-estrangement 8, 12, 82, 124, 126–7, 130
   subject of embodiment 19–20
   use value 54
hybridity
   animal and technology (prosthesis) 2, 4, 121
   animal and the automation of signification 12, 24, 27, 57–9
   non-human as hybrid 65, 128, 130
   hybrid or the radical dyad 128 (*see also* radical dyad)

idealism 9, 13, 22, 26, 39, 49
identity 10–13, 32, 34, 42–5, 64–5, 71, 74, 77–80, 84, 86–7, 102–7, 122
   as fetish 37, 44, 115–16, 120, 124
   last instance 23, 34, 42, 44–5, 59–62
   as reification 37, 118
idiot 138–9
inhuman 2–4, 11, 24, 27, 44, 117, 121, 123–4, 128–9. *See also* cyborg; nonhuman
inanity 4
inhumanity 3–4, 11, 24, 27, 44, 121, 123–4, 128–9
intelligence 50, 62–4, 68, 76
   artificial 62, 71, 105
   excarnate 43
   pretentiousness of 50
Irigaray, Luce 26, 34, 36, 44, 73, 113–15, 122, 124
   capital and patriarchy as exchange of women 26, 36, 44, 122
   Speculum of the Other Woman 37, 115
   This Sex Which Is Not One 113, 115

Kant, Immanuel, *noumenon* 26
knowledge 4, 6, 11, 14–16, 64, 68, 78, 85, 99, 130, 138
Kolozova, Katerina 9, 14, 52

labor/labour 19–20, 28
   abstraction 20
   agency 46

capitalist production 146
  division of 94–5
  exploitation 47
  forms of 142
  global workforce 47
  hierarchy 47
  means of 91
  power 93–4
  underpaid 19
  wage 28, 142–4, 148
labourer 93–4
Lacan, Jacques 8, 13–14, 26, 30, 39, 41, 124
  automaton, notion of 29–30, 34, 39
  psychoanalysis 41, 113, 124
language 4–6, 20–2, 24–6
  formalisation 70–3
  homologous 4, 10–11, 67
  natural 57–8
  relation with real 5–6
  as technology 58–62
Laruelle, François 13, 15–17, 25–6. See also radical dyad
  on dualysis procesdure 5–6, 21
  human-in-human, notion of 4–5, 59, 70, 72, 125–6
  "idempotency" 44
  Introduction to Non-Marxism 7, 10–11, 60, 81, 97
  non-philosophical method 7, 22
  "philo-fiction" 26
  "philosophical impoverishment" 39, 79, 81, 105–11
  "philosophical spontaneity" 2, 6, 34, 103–4
  "Pour une linguistique active (la notion de phonèse)" 33
  "principle of sufficient philosophy" or PSP 13, 40, 49, 85, 106, 136
  "Theory of the Strangers" 124, 126
  phonesis 34
  Theory of Identities 61
  truth vs real 5–7, 39–40
  unilaterality (or "the Vision-in-One") 22

last instance, determination of 6, 9, 17, 18, 21–2, 24. See also real; wage labor
  abolishment of animal for killing 139, 142, 145–6
  automata of capital and patriarchy 114–17, 126, 128
  identity, of/in the last instance 23, 34, 42, 44–5, 59–62
  identity, as fetish 37, 44, 115–16, 120, 124
  identity, as reification 37, 118
  materialist reason 61–2, 72, 78–9, 83–4, 86–7
  radical dyad 30, 35, 45, 50–1
  subjectivity 92, 103–4, 107–9
Levi-Strauss, Claude 31, 115–16
life
  automaton of 106
  body and physicality 2–3
  commodification of 3, 83
  exploitation 108, 110
  meaning and value 125–6
Loffler, Davor 6, 45, 130

machines 3, 12, 29, 46–7, 62, 68, 86, 94, 127, 129, 142, 148–50
  animals as 148–50
  capitalist automaton 91–2
  origin and power 58–60
Mackenzie, Lewis, M., *Computation and Its Limits* 63
marriage exchange 27, 121–2
Marx, Karl
  on atomism 101
  class consciousness 47–8
  Critique of Hegel's Philosophy in General 10, 14, 90, 92, 100–1, 105, 127–8, 137, 140
  Critique of Political Economy 95, 100, 103
  Economic-Philosophic Manuscripts 1844 48, 52, 140
  epistemic choice 9
  Estranged Labour 15

first affirmation 129–33 (*See also* xeno
    feminism)
  on forms of "Universal Egoist" 26
  on general category of the animal
    146–51
  German Ideology, Part 1: Feuerbach 101
  German Ideology and *Philosophical
    Economic Manuscripts 1844*
    89–90, 99
  *Grundrisse: Foundation of the Critique
    of Political Economy* 101, 103–4
  *Grundrisse: Outlines of the Critique of
    Political Economy* 90–1
  "Manifesto of the Communist Party,"
    7–8, 94, 118
  on materialism 103
  materialist formalism 25
  naturalism and humanism 48
  on ownership of private property 47–8
  *Philosophical-Economic Manuscripts
    1884* 7, 90
  political economy 35, 41
  "Private Property and Communism"
    8, 82
  question of subjectivity 89–90
  "species being of humanity" 15, 28, 38,
    59–60, 66, 79, 81, 83, 96, 100,
    123–4, 127, 130, 139, 150
  Theses on Feuerbach and *Critique of
    Hegel's Philosophy* 8, 10, 14,
    26, 49, 90, 92, 98, 100–1, 105,
    127–8, 137, 140
masculinity 37, 78–9, 114–16, 118, 121
material
  automaton process 106–9, 116, 123
  capitalist machine 18–23
  continuity 24, 124, 126–7, 141
  Marx's view 55–8
  philosophical 6–7, 10, 55–6, 73–4, 104
  production 9–10, 18, 48
  reality 9, 16, 25
  transcendental 6, 38–9, 61, 65, 72, 122
  use 18
  value production 125

materialism 8–9, 48–9, 52, 90, 122, 137
materiality 11–12, 16–17, 19–20, 23–4,
    35–6, 42, 44–6, 57–9, 70–1, 79–80,
    101–2, 107, 109–10, 115–18, 120
  discrete duality 11
  of formalism 55–8
  forms of 50
  money 17
  non-human identity 42–7
  of unity 12
means of production 2, 47–8, 52, 92–3, 95,
    103, 106–7, 131
metaphysical 11, 36, 45, 50, 54, 64–7, 75,
    81, 83, 94, 114
  questions 6, 15–16, 21, 45–6, 55–6, 66–7
metaphysics 1, 15–16, 20, 28, 45, 56, 64,
    66–8, 71, 83, 94–5, 110, 119, 147
  animal for killing, abolishment 135–9
  body-machine hierarchy 20
  formalism 67–9, 74–80
Michaelson, Greg, *Computation and Its
    Limits* 63
mimesis 6, 11, 25, 38
money 17–18, 37–8, 45, 57, 71, 92, 110,
    119–20, 127
  circulations of 18–9

naturalism 8, 48, 90–1, 131, 136
natural languages 29, 43, 57–8, 61, 63–4,
    70
  categorical thinking 70–3
nature
  capitalist automation 26–7, 37, 107,
    114–15, 117, 119–20, 123, 132
  and culture 121, 123
  exploitation 95
  exteriority of philosophical reason
    105–11
  subjectivism of philosophy 90–7
non-humans
  agency of *techné* 59
  chains of destruction 142
  emancipation 148
  as non-animals 135–6, 138

post-philosophical treatment 21
radical dyad 22–5, 29, 42, 49, 124
radical hybridity 59–60, 65, 130
reality of selfhood 42–3, 45, 70–3, 127
use value 54
Non-Marxism 7, 10–11, 40–1, 60, 81, 97, 154
non-philosophy 5–7, 10–11, 13, 32, 35, 38–9, 56, 59–60, 66–7, 74, 81–2, 85, 97, 104
formalism 81–6

Ó Maoilearca, J. 44, 135–6, 138, 142
Angelaki 135
"philosomorphic" 135, 142
ontology 20, 72, 104–5, 110, 129, 133, 145

patriarchy 23–6, 28–9, 36–7, 44, 57, 64, 80, 113–17, 119–23, 125, 127, 129, 131–3, 147
automata of 26–7, 37, 113–15, 116, 119–20, 122, 132
as exchange of phallic power 29
Paul Smith, Anthony 105
philosophy 6–8, 13–17, 19–22, 25–8
physicality 6–8, 13–17, 19–22, 25–8, 38–40, 42–5, 89–90, 96–8, 100–1, 126–30, 132–3, 135–9, 147–8
questions of intelligence 62–6
sense of alienation 123–9
subjectivism 90–7
subjectivity 98–105
physicality 2, 9–12, 19–20, 37, 39–41, 43–6, 49, 68, 71, 84–6, 101, 105–10, 114–15, 117, 120, 125–8, 130–2, 149–50. *See also* last instance, determination of
automaton 11–13, 18–24, 26–35, 37, 39–41, 49–53, 56–60, 68–72, 82–6, 90–2, 102–7, 116–20, 122–4, 149–50
capitalism 16–17, 19, 21, 23–6, 28, 42, 45–7, 54, 93–5, 109–10, 130–1, 142, 144, 147

philosophy 6–8, 13–17, 19–22, 25–8, 38–40, 42–5, 89–90, 96–8, 100–1, 126–30, 132–3, 135–9, 147–8
subjectivity 3, 5, 20, 24, 26, 64–5, 89–93, 98–105, 113, 117, 126, 128, 130, 133, 136, 138, 140–2
Plato
mythology of the *eidon* 52
Timaeus 37, 117, 120
political economy 10, 23, 25, 36, 41, 47, 81–2, 89, 108, 110, 125, 147
of capitalism 147
Marx's view 25, 35, 41, 82, 89
possibilities for new 135–51
status of subjectivities 47
post-humanism
animals 2
automation 4
categories 86
contemporary 3
human decentering 138, 148
last instance, identification of 102–3
non-anthropocentric 103
non-human identity 12
technological enhancement 3
visions of society 1–3
Wolfe, Cary on 46
post-structuralism 4, 14–15, 53
Power, Nina 132–3, 150
Preconditions 20, 27, 52–3, 57, 71, 109, 122, 132
principle of sufficient philosophy (*PSP*) 13, 40, 49, 85, 106, 136
psychoanalysis 7, 25, 39, 41–2, 104

quantum theory
non-philosophical and non-Marxist formalisation 40
superposition method 25, 136, 145

radical dyad. *See also* animal; technology
categories of real 34–42
individual, subjection and exploitation 47–54

last instance, determination of 6, 30, 35, 45, 50–1
materiality of 42–7
nonhuman identity 1, 3–4, 11–12, 20–1, 23–5, 27, 29, 31, 35, 42, 44–5, 49–50, 54, 59–60, 65, 70–2, 86, 102, 114, 124, 126–7, 130, 135–6, 138, 142, 145, 148
philosophical amphibology 38, 125, 150
reality of selfhood 42–7
radical metaphysics 52, 67–8, 77, 82, 84
rationalism 37, 72, 129–30, 133
real
  abstraction 10, 35, 51, 56–8, 61, 69, 71, 73, 79–80, 84, 128, 147
  exteriority 5–6, 13–15, 21, 30, 44–5, 61, 71, 82, 123–4, 128, 136–7
  thought and 5–6, 11, 13–16, 24–5, 35, 38, 40, 49, 66, 137, 146–7, 150
realism 7, 9–10, 21
reality, physical 30–1, 44, 52, 56, 58, 94, 106, 128
reification 16, 35–6, 72, 127–8, 146
reproduction 78, 115–16, 132
  sexual 80, 116, 119–20
  social 38, 80, 144
Roden, David 102

Saussure, Ferdinand de 13, 25, 31–4, 39, 55, 64, 73, 80
  phonetics, scientific practice 30–1, 33–4, 39
  signification, concept of 29–30
  structuralist theory 13, 30–4
Schmid, Anne-Francoise 78
Schmitt, Carl 108
self
  concept 53
  -consciousness 98, 127–8, 148
  non-human 44–5, 70, 127
  prelingual 43, 127, 138
  -sufficiency 52, 56, 102
Sellars, W., "manifest image of reality" 40
senselessness 12–13, 24, 92, 94

sensuousness 9, 14, 16, 49, 140
sexuality 78, 116, 120, 122
  heteronormative 147
  orientation 115
  practice and identity 115–16
  queerness 120
signification 12–13, 24–7, 29–30, 32, 34–5, 38–9, 41, 43–5, 48–50, 56, 58–62, 64, 70, 75, 113–14
  automata 12–13, 34, 48, 60, 70, 82, 114, 121, 123, 126, 130
  binary model 75–6
  computerised signification 62–6
  concept 29–30
Simondon, Gilbert 101–2, 104, 106
Smith, Anthony Paul 105
socialism 52, 108
social relations 4, 9–10, 16–17, 28, 35–6, 49, 51, 54, 64, 69, 80, 123, 127–8, 139
Sohn-Rethel, Alfred 10, 35–6, 56–7, 69
species 26, 28, 30, 55, 59–60, 66, 79–81, 83, 96, 100, 123–4, 127, 130, 145–6, 150–1
Spinoza, Benedict de
  conatus 51, 68, 71, 106–7
  Ethics 51, 106–7
subjectivity
  anthropocentrism 83
  categories of 20
  determination of last instance 92, 103–4, 107–9
  new forms 3, 31
  non-objective being 16
  patriarchal agency 117
  philosophical relevance 24, 26, 85, 89–93, 98–9, 128, 130
  philosophy 98–105
  physicality 3, 5, 20, 24, 26, 64–5, 89–93, 95, 97–9, 101, 103, 105, 107, 117, 130
  pure 130, 133
  radical 124, 126, 136
  selfhood and agency 64–5

INDEX

signifying automaton 43, 64, 68, 70
structure of thought 101, 105, 140
techno-logical blending 60
third person's perspective 26, 138
sublation 12, 38, 118, 121
substance, 13, 30, 36, 41, 51, 56–7, 71, 97, 104, 109, 117, 149
surplus value
    abolition of 109
    acceleration of exchange 17–18, 52
    exploitation of life 108, 110
    fetishised abstraction 111, 117, 120
    formula 38, 82, 93, 119
    masculinity and femininity (gender determination) 37, 81, 115–16, 120–1
    means of production 95
    purchase of labour power 94
    use value *versus* 17–18, 20, 36, 48, 54, 73, 93, 144
Sussman, Gerald Jay 58, 63
syllogisms 63, 65, 68–9, 76
    Bayesian method 65
syntax 6, 61, 64, 69, 73, 83–4, 98, 106

tautology 37, 56, 75, 93, 113–15
    P(hallus)-M-C-M- M-M 18, 113–18
    tautological 23, 26, 37, 117, 120
    value as 107, 113
techné 49, 58–9, 64–6, 68, 70, 82, 130
technology
    abstraction of labor 142
    -body dyad 121, 123
    exploitation of life 110
    extension or *prosthesis* 129
    hybridisation 120
    as language 58–62
    last instance identity 65, 114, 116, 121
    Marx on 131
    as means of production 47, 52, 103, 106–7
    moral intentionality 3
    mutation of 104
    nature and 85

rationality or scientific reason 82–3
transhumanism 46
via tool and *metis* 130
theology
    essentialist naturalism 131
    philosophy and 46, 56, 131, 136
thought
    "abstract egoist" 105
    automaton 50, 60–1
    circular message 52
    formalism 73
    human centered 102
    language and 22, 69
    Laruelle on 72
    last instance 21
    level of 105, 128
    logic and operation 75
    Marx on 140
    meta-positioning 65
    "moral substance" of exploitation 23
    posture of 6, 15, 21–2, 25–6, 52, 61, 66, 73, 83, 104–5, 133
    radical metaphysical concept 74, 136–7, 139
    real and 5–6, 11, 13–16, 24–5, 35, 38, 40, 49, 66, 137, 146–7, 150
    scientific 100
    sound waves 77
    structure 101
    Vision-in-One 22, 104
Trajanoski, Zarko 14
transcendence
    masculinity 118
    of metaphysics 1, 11
    physicality 57, 59, 72
    positive 8
    posthumanism 46
    private property 5–6, 82
    real as exteriority 44
    reality 5–6, 21–2
    scientific nature 83–5, 100
    syntax of real 73
    unification of 128
    women's status 114

transformation 7, 21, 27, 46, 110, 117, 122
Turing, Alan 62–3, 65, 68
  definition of computing 62
  on machine's understanding 65
  syllogism 68
  Turing Machines (TMs) 63

unification 3, 5, 10, 12–13
unilaterality 5, 21–2, 24, 31, 35, 39, 97, 104
  internal 42
  radical 40
  relation of 31, 102
universe 17–18, 24
  self-sufficient 17, 19, 41, 51, 104

value
  definition 23
  exchange system 29, 41, 57, 64
  production 18, 28, 41, 55, 92, 107, 115, 125
  of purity 51
Vernant, Jean-Pierre 50, 50 n.3, 117
  analysis of intelligence 50
vitalism
  commodification of life 3, 83
  material continuity 125, 136–7, 149
  surplus value, creation of 93

wage labor 28, 93, 142–4, 148. *See also* animal, killing or suffering
Western religion, structures of authority 150
Williams, Donald Cary 71
Wittgenstein, Ludwig 25, 61, 74–7
  binary signification model 75–6
  idea of Maßstab 12, 23, 25, 42, 74, 76–7, 107, 139
  Tractatus Logico-Philosophicus 74
Wolfe, Cary 3, 46, 52, *What Is Posthumanism?* 3
Women. *See also* female/femaleness; gender
  animals and 142–3, 148
  exchange of 36, 44, 57, 122
  social relations 4
Wood, Allen 7
Wynter, Sylvia on classarchy 86

xeno-feminism
  complicity with capitalism 129–33
  gendered presuppositions 133
  last instance philosophy 132

Žižek, Slavoj 131

www.ingramcontent.com/pod-product-compliance
Lightning Source LLC
Chambersburg PA
CBHW052048300426
44117CB00012B/2029